JIM HEWITSON'S
SCOTTISH MISCELLANY

JIM HEWITSON'S
SCOTTISH MISCELLANY

BLACK & WHITE PUBLISHING

First published 2003
by Black & White Publishing Ltd
99 Giles Street, Edinburgh EH6 6BZ

Reprinted 2004

ISBN 1 902927 84 2

Text copyright © Jim Hewitson 2003
Illustrations copyright © John Marshall 2003

The right of Jim Hewitson to be identified
as the author of this work has been asserted
by him in accordance with the
Copyright, Designs and Patents Act 1988.

A CIP catalogue record for this book
is available from The British Library.

Cover design www.henrysteadman.com

Printed and bound by Creative Print and Design

TO LINDSEY

apprentice to the silly sorcerer

and for all those who patiently listened to my often bizarre inquiries and did not call the men in white coats. But in particular:

Alastair Bonnington, Christina Mackenzie, Alan Raeburn, Jimmy Brown, Convention of Scottish Local Authorities, Elaine Low, Aly Macdonald, Scottish Natural Heritage, Liam McIlvanney, Ronald M Douglas, Bobby Leslie, Stephen Arnott, Owen O'Leary, Ken Mutch, Catherine Walker, Linda McGowan, Ruth Neeve, David Forsyth, Helen Clark, Caroline Chinn, Fiona Marwick, Alex Robertson, Caroline Strachan, Tom Muir, Tommy Watt, Carol Anne Campbell, Noel Miller, Beverley Quinn, Sarah Barclay, Zoe Laidlaw, Fiona Harvey, Frank Hanlon, John Johnson, Rosemary Middleton, Paul Warren, Paul Jordan, Neil Greig, Elaine Fee, Barrie Cox-Dacre.

INTRODUCTION

How do you measure Scottishness? Is it in the fearsome strength of your Friday night curry or the length of the eagle feather in your bunnet? Is it the belief that Scotland must regain her role in the international community or the sobering realisation that your life is a wee bit too closely mirrored in the latest *River City* storyline?

One scary yet inspiring possibility is this – is our sense of Scottishness merely a reflection of the fact that we have not yet been fully absorbed into the uniform, featureless – frankly boring – world of Englishness?

Do you have a rampant thistle tattooed on your butt or is there a tattered copy of Rabbie Burns's poems somewhere in the house?

If you feel you do not qualify as Scottish on any of these counts, then despair not – Scottishness is a big kirk with plenty of pews. This book is for Scots born and bred, for the new Scots – whatever colour or creed and whether they hail originally from Leeds or Lahore. It's for openly wannabe Scots, closet Scots and everyone who suspects, hopes and prays that we are a nation still – and a damned interesting one at that!

JH

How to Raise the Clans

When a chieftain had a score to settle or a prince to support, the fiery cross (*crean tarigh*) came into its own. Should you ever need to summon your clansfolk for similar purposes or simply to gather folk together for a bus trip to Troon, here's how you go about it:

- Ensure you are sufficiently het up, outraged and/or thirsting for vengeance
- Make a handy-sized cross from any light wood
- Take one goat and slaughter it
- Sear the extremities of the cross in a fire
- Extinguish it with the animal's blood before relighting
- Send a fleet-of-foot messenger with the cross to the next village
- Every man from 16–60 should respond to the call
- They should proceed, fully armed, to the pre-arranged rendezvous point
- Failure to do so will incur infamy and/or a swift boot up the jacksie

During the Forty-five uprising, the fiery cross often made an appearance. It once passed through the whole district of Breadalbane in Appin, covering thirty-two miles in just three hours. Stuart of Invernahayle said he sent round the fiery cross on one occasion when two government frigates appeared offshore. All the fighting men were away with Bonnie Prince Charlie in England but, in a few hours, old folk and children answered the summons and a huge enthusiastic force had soon gathered – ready to do battle. Any idea of a landing, if it was planned for the 'county of absent warriors', was quickly abandoned by the redcoats and the frigates sailed away.

Fun's Fun
But Keep Yer Arse Oot the Sandwiches!

The splendid baptism feast of James VI at Stirling, in 1566, almost developed into a rammy when Bastian, a French servant of Mary, Queen of Scots, mischievously ordered a team of servants, disguised as satyrs (randy half-men, half-goats), to wave their tails provocatively in the faces of the English guests as they dined.

Ugly Bugs
Scotland's Top Road-Kill Victims

You probably don't want to know this but it's distinctly possible that, during our brief Scottish summer, when you take the car down to the shops for a pint of milk or the paper, you are wiping out an entire civilisation en route.

We tend to associate road kill with the more obvious victims – rabbits, foxes, cats, dogs and hedgehogs – but it is the insect population that takes the most substantial hits by a long mile – as anyone trying to wash a car bonnet or windscreen knows only too well.

INSECTS CONSUME TEN PER CENT OF THE WORLD'S FOOD PRODUCTION EVERY YEAR

IF YOU WEIGHED ALL THE INSECTS IN THE WORLD AGAINST ALL THE OTHER ANIMALS ON THE PLANET, THE INSECTS WOULD BE HEAVIER

INSECTS OUTNUMBER HUMANS BY 100 MILLION TO ONE

SCIENTISTS DISCOVER UP TO 10,000 NEW SPECIES OF INSECT EVERY YEAR

IT IS THOUGHT THAT THERE MAY BE AS MANY AS TEN MILLION UNDISCOVERED SPECIES

Statistics in this area are clearly difficult – if not impossible, in the case of the insects – to come by. A recent survey suggested that, in the UK, 274 hedgehogs, 137 badgers, 110 deer and fourteen birds of prey are fatally injured by vehicles every day. In the same period, an average of nine people are killed on the roads.

In order to get an idea of the range and proportion of animal victims of the internal combustion engine, I approached various Scottish animal-welfare and -protection groups for their impressions of the relative hit rates and this is what they came up with:

1. INSECTS	4. HEDGEHOGS	7. DEER	10. SHEEP
2. RABBITS	5. FOXES	8. BADGERS	11. CROWS/PHEASANTS
3. FROGS, TOADS	6. CATS	9. DOGS	12. VOLES, STOATS, ETC

Literature on this topic is fairly thin on the ground but *The Totaled Roadkill Cookbook*, by an American gent called Buck Petersen, offers such tasteless culinary delights as 'Hush Puppies', 'Winshiel Wabbits' and 'Highway Hash'.

Just occasionally, we encounter stories that display a kind of reassuring concern for the plight of animal road users. Recently, part of Queen's Drive in Edinburgh was closed off for two weeks after the number of amphibians being squashed by cars had reached record proportions. The move was designed to protect female toads migrating from damp grassland to Holyrood Park's deep ponds to mate.

The De'il Tak' the Hin'most

Scotland has had what can only be described as an uncanny relationship with Satan over the years. In a country which, for centuries, was so hung up on the consequences of improper or immoral behaviour, we seem to have an almost lightsome association with the Proprietor of Hades – especially when you consider that so many of us should, realistically, be anticipating a long-stay ticket in his hot zone. Here are a few essential pieces of satanic Scottish lore:

SATAN HAS A WHEEN OF NICKNAMES AMONGST THE SCOTS. THEY INCLUDE:
THE DE'IL • THE MASTER OF WITCHES • THE EVIL ONE
DÒMHNULL DUBH (BLACK DONALD)
THE TRICKY RASCAL • AULD CLOOTIE
NICK HORNIE • THE EARL O' HELL
THE LAIRD O' YON PLACE
THE QUEER FELLA

IN SCOTTISH REPORTS OF OCCASIONS WHEN THE DEVIL PUTS IN APPEARANCE, HE IS NORMALLY DESCRIBED AS A BEAST-MAN COMPLETE WITH HORNS, FIRE-FLAMING HAIR, BLACK-SPOTTED RED FACE AND A BODY ENCASED IN SCALES. MIGHT BE DIFFICULT TO SPOT HIM IN THE SATURDAY NIGHT PUB OR CLUB?

SURELY THE MOST SINISTER PORTRAYAL OF AULD NICK COMES IN JAMES HOGG'S INFINITELY SOMBRE *THE PRIVATE MEMOIRS AND CONFESSIONS OF A JUSTIFIED SINNER* (1824) WITH THE CHARACTER OF GILMARTIN JUST GUARANTEED TO GIVE YOU THE HEEBIE-JEEBIES.

THERE IS NO RECORD OF THE DEVIL HAVING APPEARED WEARING THE KILT. (DOES THIS SUGGEST THAT HE IS MOST PROBABLY OF THE LOWLAND PERSUASION?)

SO SPECTACULAR WAS THE PLAYING STYLE OF GENOESE VIOLINIST PAGANINI THAT, WHEN HE VISITED GLASGOW IN 1831, KIRK MINISTERS DEMANDED A BOYCOTT BECAUSE IT WAS SAID THAT THE VIOLINIST HAD ENTERED INTO A PACT WITH SATAN. THE PRAGMATIC GLASWEGIANS WERE NOT IMPRESSED AND PACKED HIS PERFORMANCES.

JUST OCCASIONALLY THE DEVIL CAN APPEAR AS A HANDSOME YOUNG MAN – MOSTLY CLOTHED BUT, FROM TIME TO TIME, IN THE BUFF.

THE DEVIL OF THE SCOTS HAS ALWAYS DISPLAYED A LIKING FOR THE BAGPIPES, A WEE REFRESHMENT AND A WHIRL ROUND THE DANCE FLOOR – A CASE OF WHEN IN ROME OR ROTHESAY . . .

IN A VERY CIVILISED MANNER, HE DOES NOT, IN HIS AMOROUS CALEDONIAN ADVENTURES, DISTINGUISH BETWEEN FRESH-FACED LASSES AND WIZENED OCTOGENARIANS. HIS FAVOURS ARE WIDELY SPREAD.

AULD NICK WAS PERHAPS SCOTLAND'S MOST SINISTER LANDLORD. IN 1594, THE FATHERS OF THE REFORMATION ORDERED AN END TO THE CENTURIES'-OLD TRADITION WHICH DEMANDED THAT A PIECE OF LAND ON EVERY FARM, KNOWN AS 'THE GUIDMAN'S CROFT' SHOULD BE LEFT UNTILLED IN RECOGNITION OF THE INFLUENCE OF THE DEVIL. AND, EVEN TODAY, ON SOME FARMS, YOU'LL FIND SMALL PATCHES OF SEEMINGLY FERTILE GROUND INEXPLICABLY UNCULTIVATED.

NO MATTER HOW CLEVERLY THE DEVIL DISGUISES HIMSELF – AS A YOUNG MAN OR AS A SCABBY BEAST – HIS CLOVEN HOOVES ARE ALWAYS IN EVIDENCE.

DURING THE CLEARANCES IN THE FIRST HALF OF THE NINETEENTH CENTURY, IT WAS SUGGESTED THAT THE DEVIL HAD SET UP AN ACADEMY OF EVIL IN ORDER TO TEACH THE PRINCIPAL CHIEFS AND LAIRDS HOW TO BE NASTY. IN RETROSPECT, HE WAS CLEARLY AN ABLE DOMINIE WITH SOME PARTICULARLY WILLING PUPILS.

HOOFNOTE: Forget all those silly tales about hanging horseshoes with the open ends uppermost to 'keep in the luck'. This is an English precaution, I suspect. In Scotland, they can be hung any way you choose because they're not good luck charms at all but devices for warding off evil. The background to this special arrangement of ours concerns a Lochaber blacksmith and a midnight visit from the de'il who was badly in need of shoeing. The sleepy smith accidentally drove a nail in to the fleshy part of Auld Nick's hoof. Hopping around like a dementit thing, the devil granted the smith any wish if he would just remove the nail. The deal struck was that, wherever a horseshoe lay or was hung, nothing evil could pass.

Getting Mary on Film

The Execution of Mary, Queen of Scots, a pioneering motion picture made in 1895 in New Jersey, is said to have been the first to use actors. Star of this costume drama was Mr R L Thomas who played Mary – no place yet for any budding Cameron Diaz.

John Ford's 1936 movie about Mary, Queen of Scots had the late Katherine Hepburn cast as the tragic queen but it was a troubled film with a number of on-set confrontations. It was clear to most observers that, despite her initial enthusiasm, Hepburn (who claimed to be a descendant of Mary's third husband, James Hepburn, Earl of Bothwell) was uninspired. She was to admit later, 'I can't stand Mary of Scotland. I think she was an absolute ass. I would have loved to play Elizabeth – now she was a fascinating creature. But I have no patience with Mary, I thought Elizabeth was absolutely right to have her condemned to death.' Hardly the right frame of mind to give a memorable portrayal.

'The Wee Cock Sparra'

Hogmanay TV in the 1950s was full of delightfully predictable ingredients which reminded us of family, continuity, simple pleasures. It was a slower more thoughtful world when there was time to laugh and cry. No Hogmanay black-and-white TV fest would have been complete without Duncan Macrae's gloomy and wonderful interpretation of the traditional Scots song, 'The Wee Cock Sparra'. The skill in presenting this particular ditty is to build the tension and the excitement in the repeated lines. You might have heard big Duncan recite this 1000 times but it never lost its moody melodrama.

A WEE COCK SPARRA

A WEE COCK SPARRA SAT ON A TREE,
A WEE COCK SPARRA SAT ON A TREE,
A WEE COCK SPARRA SAT ON A TREE,
CHIRPIN AWA AS BLITHE AS COULD BE.

ALANG CAME A BOY WI A BOW AND AN ARRA,
ALANG CAME A BOY WI A BOW AND AN ARRA,
ALANG CAME A BOY WI A BOW AND AN ARRA,
AND HE SAID, 'I'LL GET YE, YE WEE COCK SPARRA.'

THE BOY WI THE ARRA LET FLY AT THE SPARRA,
THE BOY WI THE ARRA LET FLY AT THE SPARRA,
THE BOY WI THE ARRA LET FLY AT THE SPARRA,
AND HE HIT A MAN THAT WAS HURLIN A BARRA.

THE MAN WI THE BARRA CAM OWRE WI THE ARRA,
THE MAN WI THE BARRA CAM OWRE WI THE ARRA,
THE MAN WI THE BARRA CAM OWRE WI THE ARRA,
AND SAID, 'YE TAK ME FOR A WEE COCK SPARRA?'

THE MAN HIT THE BOY, THOUGH HE WISNAE HIS FARRA,
THE MAN HIT THE BOY, THOUGH HE WISNAE HIS FARRA,
THE MAN HIT THE BOY, THOUGH HE WISNAE HIS FARRA,
AND THE BOY STOOD AND GLOWER'D – HE WAS HURT TAE THE MARRA.

AND A THIS TIME THE WEE COCK SPARRA,
AND A THIS TIME THE WEE COCK SPARRA,
AND A THIS TIME THE WEE COCK SPARRA,
WAS CHIRPIN AWA ON THE SHANK O THE BARRA.

Okay, this will confirm, for anyone under the age of twenty, that the post-war generation are so seriously uncool as to be almost medieval. Far be it from me to advocate the use of alcohol but this is one song that somehow suddenly comes to life with suitable lubrication.

The Grey, Orange and Green Areas of History

It's one of the oddities of history that, in the aftermath of the Battle of the Boyne in 1690 – a Protestant victory over Catholic forces and one remembered (at least by the legions locked in the past) with mixed emotions in the West of Scotland to this day – Pope Alexander VIII ordered a peal of bells to be rung in celebration. Yes, you did read that correctly – to celebrate a Protestant success for William of Orange over the Catholic army of James VII, the pope ordered the bells to be rung in celebration. The bigger picture, however, was that the battle was one of several in the War of the Grand Alliance (1688–98) and was seen, throughout Europe – including the Vatican – as a victory against the allies of the French who, at this time, were trying to sever the French Catholic Church's dependence on Rome.

A Crying Shame

The pebbles on the holy shores of Iona are said to be the salt tears of a mermaid who, after falling for one of the top monks, was refused a human heart and a human soul.

Continental Insults

When umbrellas appeared for the first time in the streets of Edinburgh and Glasgow their use was frowned on. Gamps were seen as ungodly, uncouth and, worst of all, a continental affectation. The ultimate insult hurled at one of the brolly-wielding innovators was – 'Frenchman!'

The Soliloquy with the Fringe on Top

It is surely one of the modern Scottish miracles that the world's greatest celebration of wackiness and the most outrageous fanfare of the bizarre, the Edinburgh Festival Fringe, should be staged in a country so strait-laced that, not so many years ago, a French visitor, strolling back from church, was told to ease back on the pace lest folk thought he was taking a walk. In 2003, the number of Fringe venues topped the 200 mark for the first time and you might have seen the following:

A DANCE GROUP PADDLING THEIR STUFF BENEATH AN ARTIFICIAL WATERFALL

A THEATRE GROUP PERFORMING THEIR SHOW, ENTITLED *LADIES AND GENTS*, IN A PUBLIC TOILET BEHIND THE ST JAMES CENTRE

COMEDIAN ALFIE JOEY ENTERTAINING AN AUDIENCE OF FOUR EVERY AFTERNOON IN HIS RED FORD ESCORT

A SHOW CALLED *TOAST* BEING STAGED ON THE RUNGS OF A STEPLADDER

ANOTHER COMPANY PERFORMING *HAMLET* FROM THE TOP OF A TELEPHONE BOX IN THE ROYAL MILE

Scrapping in Their Simmets

In 1544, a clan battle in the Great Glen was fought in the midst of a July heatwave. The clansmen – Frasers facing up to Camerons and Donalds – stripped to their long shirts and fought throughout the hot day. Hundreds died in what became known in the folk tales as 'The Battle of the Shirts'.

Some Nifty Pipe/Fiddle/Dance Tune Titles and Dedications

'The Doon Hingin' Tie' was composed by Iain Peterson for legendary fiddler and composer, the late Dr Tom Anderson of Lerwick, to mark the occasion when Tom arrived at a royal garden party wearing an ordinary tie when everyone else was wearing a bow tie.

'*Moladh an Ruis air a Phraidheagh le Cneamh's Uisge Beatha*' was written by the band Cantrip's piper, Dan Houghton. The Gaelic title translates as 'In Praise of the Whisky and Garlic Fried Rice' and apparently celebrates a concoction produced at the end of a hard week of recording. Says Dan, 'We discovered that the edible contents of the kitchen consisted of a bulb of garlic, half a bottle of whisky, leftover rice and an egg. We cooked it all together in a wok – delicious!'

Rory Campbell named the pipe tune 'Even in the Rain' in honour of an impressive statue, that stands in the Midlothian village of Loanhead, of a man grooming a horse. The stony groom continues his work unfazed by wind, snow and rain.

Fiddler Gillian Frame wrote a tune called 'Spider Legs' for a Glasgow taxi driver who, whilst approaching traffic lights at high speed playing a harmonica, had given too much information about what he looked like in a kilt.

Orcadian piper Andy Cant, of the group Three Piece Suite, was so moved when he learned that BBC Radio Orkney senior producer John Fergusson had been admitted to hospital, suffering from kidney problems, that he penned his 'Lament for the Passing of John Fergusson's Kidney Stone'.

Two pipe tunes, 'The Clumsy Lover' by Neil Dickie and 'The Successful Lover' by Alan MacDonald, celebrate very different romantic encounters. The latter was written as a positive counterpoint to Neil's original.

As a tribute to all those worthy folk who race around trying and failing to manage life's crises, Paul Warren, of the National Piping Centre in Glasgow, wrote 'The Heedless Chicken Jig'.

Simon Bradley composed a tune called 'The Fiddle Cushion'. The melody marks the occasion, in an Edinburgh bar, when Simon sat on a fiddle belonging to his namesake, Simon Thoumire.

After a suggestion by his fellow band member that they should use kangaroo-skin bags for their pipes, Chris Armstrong wrote a wee tune called 'Bushtucker Man'. Chris has a bit of a forte for obscure titles. Among his other compositions are: 'The Helipad', written in honour of a bald acquaintance; 'Hoover-Happy Irene', a tribute to his mum and her obsession with cleaning; and the enigmatic 'Where the Folk in Hell Sat'. Try saying that last one quickly and you'll get the effect.

'The Inside Oot Fish Eater' was composed by Peter Wood for his fellow bandleader Lindsay Weir who has the unusual technique of eating a fish supper from the centre outwards.

MAKE WHAT YOU WILL OF THIS BATCH OF ENIGMATIC TITLES:

'THE LONG DISTANCE LOVE THRUSTER' (K QUAIL)
'THE BACK PEDDLING MUDGUARD' (A AINSWORTH)
'THE FORTY-SIX SECONDER' (F BARBOUR)
'GINGERHOG'S NO. 2' (P CUNNINGHAM)
'THE BOMBARDIER BEETLE' (P CUNNINGHAM)
'THE DRUNKEN CRUICK AND DUKE' (G MITCHELL)
'DUNCAN CHRISTIE WHO ELSE?' (G MITCHELL)
'THE BITTER LEMON REEL' (G MITCHELL)
'JACK'S POCKET ASHTRAY' (G EDWARDSON)
'ANDREW'S NEVER AS OLD AS TERRY' (M JOHNSTONE)

A Selection of Overseas Scots Town Names

Note the careless mislaying of the last letter of both Edinburgh and Glasgow by our American cousins. I suppose they are at least even-handed about it.

Glasgow	GLASGO	Kansas and Kentucky
	GLASGOW	Jamaica, Delaware, Kentucky, Missouri, Montana, Virginia
Edinburgh	EDINBORO	Pennsylvania
	EDINBURG	Illinois, Indiana, Mississippi, North Dakota, Texas, Virginia
Dundee		Nova Scotia, South Africa, Kentucky, Mississippi, Minnesota (you know the one, near Heron Lake), New York, Ohio
Aberdeen		South Africa, Idaho, Kentucky, Maryland, Mississippi, North Carolina, Ohio, South Dakota, Washington State, Hong Kong
Perth		Tasmania, Western Australia, Ontario, New Jersey (Perth Amboy)
Inverness		Nova Scotia, California, Florida, Mississippi

. . . AND A FEW MORE

1. *Airdrie, Alberta*
2. *Dumfries, Grenada*
3. *Aberfeldy, Victoria*
4. *Aberfoyle, New South Wales*
5. *Greenock, South Australia*
6. *Kirkcaldy, Alberta*

Scotland in the Skud

Scotland's only official nudist bathing beach is on the secluded Isle of Arran in the Clyde estuary but rampant unofficial skinny-dipping has been reported all over the country in recent years.

Two of the most popular stretches of coast for naturists to romp are north of Aberdeen on the miles of golden towards Balmedie and the coves and inlets of East Lothian.

The most famous naturist event in recent years was unquestionably the terrifying sight of Billy Connolly in the buff skipping among Orkney's standing stones for his TV series. Orkney had never seen the likes since the days, a thousand years ago, when Olaf Bare-Arse used to make his way home across the moors from the Stromness Steamhouse and Massage Parlour.

Scotland's first nude skier was spotted in 1974 at Carrbridge. This young man, wearing only ski boots, emerged on a day of warm sunshine.

Seamen, who seem to have almost as many superstitions as footballers, were never averse to a bit of nudity on board ship. A naked woman was said to calm the sea, hence the many wooden figureheads featuring bare-breasted beauties. Ironically, if a bare-footed woman crossed their path as the boys set off for the fishing they simply refused to go to sea.

And now we have the phenomenon of the naked rambler — a bit of a misnomer, if you ask me, as he was reported to be wearing hiking boots and a floppy hat. While he journeyed from Land's End to John o'Groats, he was only fully clad at his many court appearances to face charges of breach of the peace.

🎥 Harry Lauder's Got a Lot to Answer For 🎥

Scotland's ethnic mix grows more varied and colourful with every passing month. We are now a nation of many creeds and colours but sadly the traditional Scottish stereotype still appears on far too regular a basis in movies, books and TV.

Kilted Harry Lauder with his knock knees and crooked crummock and James Finlayson, the cross-eyed loose cannon in the Laurel and Hardy films, set the ball rolling. The moviemakers have never looked back. Still, a nation that can laugh at itself must have something going for it. If you want an example of a place which takes itself far too seriously, just keek o'er the dyke at Berwick. On conducting a straw poll of my culturally and nationalistically tuned-in acquaintances, the following were seen as the most painful or outrageous Scottish characters/accents to hit the screen. You will have candidates of your own.

1. EDWARD WOODWARD, CLOSE TO A BASKET CASE, IN *THE WICKER MAN*

2. *THE SIMPSONS'* GINGER-HAIRED JANITOR/GROUNDSMAN, WULLIE, WHOSE GRANNY CLEARLY CAME FROM AIRDRIE

3. FAT BASTARD, THE FARTING, BELCHING BOND ALTER EGO, FROM *THE SPY WHO SHAGGED ME*

4. MEL 'AH LUV YE' GIBSON MAKING MORE THAN THE ENGLISH THINK AGAIN IN *BRAVEHEART*

5. SCOTTY THE DOG IN *LADY AND THE TRAMP* WHOSE ACCENT IS RUFF TO VERY RUFF

6. BELA LUGOSI MAKING A BURKE OF HIMSELF IN *THE BODYSNATCHERS*

7. SCROOGE 'AYE, LADDIE' MCDUCK, FAMED DISNEY COIN DIVER AND CARNEGIE CLONE

8. KATHERINE HEPBURN UNCONVINCING AND HEADING FOR THE CHOP IN *MARY OF SCOTLAND*

9. ERROL 'IS THAT A SWORD I SEE BEFORE ME OR ARE YOU JUST PLEASED TO SEE ME' FLYNN IN *THE MASTER OF BALLANTRAE*

10. SHREK, THE GALLUS GREEN SCOTTISH OGRE IN THE TARTAN TIGHTS IN THE AWARD-WINNING ANIMATION

The Randy Lass o' Brechin

John Taylor, the so-called English 'water-poet', got a little more than bargained for when he visited Brechin during his famous 1618 walkabout Britain. After a hike from Deeside, he settled down in a local hostelry only to be plagued by a deaf-mute girl who insisted on climbing into bed with him. Taylor described how she was 'well-shouldered beneath the weaist' (interesting descriptive work) but he was so knackered after his trek he was unable to exploit the situation and, after shoving her into the corridor, jammed the door closed with a stout chair.

Par-Grilled Victim of the New Order

The forgotten victim of the great debate over Union with England in 1706 was the Duke of Queensberry's scullion or kitchen boy. Lord Drumlanrig, the grown son of the Duke, was a dangerous madman who was trailed around with the family and kept locked in cellars for security. During a disturbance outside the family house in Edinburgh between troops and anti-Union protestors, he was left alone while people rushed outside to watch the action. He escaped and roasted the scullion boy on the kitchen spit.

Pocket Version of the Treaty of Union, 25 March, 1707

THE TWO KINGDOMS SHOULD, AFTER THE 1ST OF MAY (1707), BE FOR EVER AFTER UNITED INTO ONE KINGDOM BY THE NAME OF GREAT BRITAIN

SUCCESSION TO THE MONARCH OF THE UNITED KINGDOM OF GREAT BRITAIN SHOULD DESCEND TO THE ELECTRESS SOPHIA OF HANOVER, AND HER HEIRS BEING PROTESTANT

THE UNITED KINGDOM SHOULD BE REPRESENTED BY ONE AND THE SAME PARLIAMENT, TO BE STYLED THE PARLIAMENT OF GREAT BRITAIN

ALL SUBJECTS OF THE UNITED KINGDOM SHOULD, FROM AND AFTER THE UNION, HAVE FULL FREEDOM OF TRADE WITHIN THE SAID UNITED KINGDOM

ALL SHIPS OR VESSELS BELONGING TO SCOTSMEN, THOUGH FOREIGN BUILT, SHOULD BE DEEMED AND PASSED AS SHIPS OF GREAT BRITAIN

ALL PARTS OF THE UNITED KINGDOM SHOULD HAVE THE SAME COMMERCIAL ALLOWANCES, ENCOURAGEMENTS AND DRAWBACKS AND BE UNDER THE SAME PROHIBITIONS, RESTRICTIONS AND REGULATIONS OF TRADE AND LIABLE TO THE SAME DUTIES ON IMPORT AND EXPORT

SCOTLAND SHALL NOT BE CHARGED WITH DUTIES PAYABLE IN ENGLAND ON WINDOWS AND LIGHTS

ALL PARTS OF THE UNITED KINGDOM SHOULD BE LIABLE TO THE
SAME EXCISE UPON ALL EXCISABLE
LIQUORS, WITH THE EXCEPTION OF BEER
OR ALE, IN WHICH THE ADVANTAGE
SHALL BE GIVEN TO THE SCOTS

ALL FOREIGN SALT IMPORTED INTO SCOTLAND SHALL BE CHARGED
THE SAME DUTIES AS ENGLAND BUT FOR
SEVEN YEARS SCOTLAND IS EXEMPTED
FROM DUTY ON HOME-PRODUCED SALT;
CHIEFLY TO ENCOURAGE SCOTTISH
FISHERIES

WHEN THE SUM OF £1,997,763 SHOULD BE DECREED BY
PARLIAMENT TO BE RAISED IN
ENGLAND AS A LAND-TAX, SCOTLAND
SHALL BE CHARGED BY THE SAME ACT
WITH THE SUM OF £48,000 AS ITS
QUOTA

SCOTLAND SHALL NOT BE CHARGED WITH THE SAME DUTIES ON
STAMPED PAPER, VELLUM AND
PARCHMENT WHICH ARE IN FORCE IN
ENGLAND

SCOTLAND TO PAY NO DUTIES ON COALS, CULM OR CINDERS
CONSUMED IN THE HOME MARKET

NO OTHER DUTIES OTHER THAN THOSE AGREED IN THE TREATY

SCOTLAND SHALL HAVE AN EQUIVALENT FOR WHAT HER SUBJECTS
SHALL BE CHARGED TOWARDS PAYMENT
OF THE DEBTS OF ENGLAND –
£398,085.10/-

COIN SHALL BE OF THE SAME STANDARD AND VALUE THROUGHOUT
THE UNITED KINGDOM

No duty in Scotland on malt

Same weights and measures are to be used throughout the United Kingdom

Laws concerning trade, customs and excise to be the same in Scotland as in England

The Court of Session to remain within Scotland, as it is now constituted by the laws of that kingdom

All heritable offices be reserved to the owners as they are now enjoyed by the laws of Scotland

The rights and privileges of the royal burghs in Scotland remain entire after Union

Of the peers of Scotland, sixteen shall be the number to sit and vote in the House of Lords and forty-five the number of representatives of Scotland in the House of Commons

The sixteen Scottish peers shall have the privileges which the peers of England now have

After the Union there is to be one Great Seal for the United Kingdom.

That all laws contrary to or inconsistent with the terms of these articles shall cease and become void

Morag's Magical Scottish Kitchen
Orkney Duff

2 cups plain flour sifted	1 cup of margarine
1 tsp baking soda	1 tsp dried cinnamon
1 tsp dried mixed spice	$^1/_2$ tsp dried ginger
1 cup granulated or castor sugar	1 tbsp syrup
1 tbsp treacle	1 cup of raisins
1 cup of sultanas	1 egg, beaten
milk to mix	2–3 oz breadcrumbs (optional)

Put the flour in a large bowl and rub in the margarine until the mixture resembles breadcrumbs. Stir in the baking soda, spices, sugar, syrup, treacle and fruit and the beaten egg. Add enough milk to create a consistency between sticky and dropping.

Scald a cloth (it's usual to use an old pillowcase for this) and lay it on the table or worktop. Dust it evenly with a layer of caster sugar followed by a layer of plain flour. Do this for an area bigger than the base of the pudding so that a skin can form on the sides and top. Place the pudding mixture in the middle of the cloth and dust lightly with some more flour. Draw up the sides of the cloth and secure it tightly with a piece of string, allowing 1–2 inches between the pudding and the top of the cloth to let the mixture expand.

Put the pudding, with the knot uppermost, into a pot of boiling water where you have previously set a heat-resistant plate in the bottom to keep the pudding from too fierce a heat. Boil the pudding for $2^1/_2$ hours, topping up regularly with boiling water and taking great care not to allow it to boil dry.

When cooked, remove the cloth from the pudding and serve it hot with custard or cream. Alternatively, allow it to cool and serve it sliced with tea or coffee.

(See p. 150 for a variation on this theme.)

Runners in the 1291 'Great Cause' Stakes at Berwick for the King's Caledonian Cup

Between 1290 and 1292 a remarkable competition unfolded for the succession to the Scottish throne following the death of the infant Margaret of Norway, on her way from Norway to take the throne (from seasickness, some say). Whatever the cause, her death signalled a rush by all sorts of nobs, nonentities and wannabes seeking the Scottish throne. Recently, in a remarkable historical discovery, the Scottish penchant for betting on anything that moves has been confirmed.

Within the walls of Berwick, a cache of documents was found to contain what is clearly a form guide to the 'Cause'. For the more imaginative amongst us, this has confirmed persistent stories that 'Honest' Tam McGilter did, indeed, operate a bookie's shop in the Border town around the end of the thirteenth century but crashed out of business after the Great Cause when Balliol, the favourite, romped home. Technical advice has kindly been offered on this feature by Dr Aly Macdonald of the University of Aberdeen's School of History.

Notes to table of runners and riders and a caveat (opposite)

Footnotes (to history)

[1] Claim based on treating the kingdom as a barony, that is, a partible inheritance between the three heirs through the female line

[2] Claim was based on documentary evidence alleged to exist but never produced (probably because it did not, in fact, exist)

[3] Claim based on ascent of claim from his daughter, the Maid of Norway, rather than descent

---

Vital note to punters:

Edward I owns the racecourse, the betting shops and most of the runners. His decision on the outcome will be final.

Runners   Odds   Tipster's Comments

Runners	Odds	Tipster's Comments
John Balliol	Even money	Hot favourite. Pedigree is excellent and has well-placed backers. Could go far. But maybe not that far
Robert Bruce	2–1	The distance may be too short for Bruce on this outing but there is great staying power in the stable
John Hastings	12–1	A dangerous outsider. His best hope is that the cup is melted down and offered as a three-way prize [1]
Florence, Count of Holland	50–1	Seems to be a strong contender according to the word from his stable. Would almost certainly fail a drugs test if victorious[2]; and, anyway, you can hardly have somebody called 'Florence' winning the 'King's Cup'
Edward I	66–1	Unlikely to win the race today but there is a suspicion that some shrewd punts will see the cup end up in the Plantagenet trophy room in any case
King Eric II of Norway	100–1	A late entrant who will attempt to win the race running backwards[3]. An outsider
John Comyn of Badenoch	500–1	Doesn't have the legs at this distance, so much so that the stable is heavily backing another runner
Robert de Pinkeny	1000–1	A no-hoper
Patrick Dunbar, Earl of March	1000–1	Another no-hoper
William de Vescy	1000–1	Why bother entering?
William de Ros	1000–1	Don't waste your money
Nicholas de Soules	1000–1	Forget it
Patrick Golightly	1000–1	Just here for the beer
Roger de Mandeville	1000–1	Unlikely even to get past the starting-post

Water Magic

St Tredwell's Chapel on my home island of Papa Westray was, in centuries past, doubly famous. It was seen as a place where, by following certain rituals such as walking around the perimeter of the loch several times in total silence, all sorts of wonderful cures could be achieved. Much more spookily, in the 1500s and 1600s, the loch also had the reputation as a place of prophecy. It is said that it had the habit of turning red (surprisingly not royal blue!) whenever anything was about to happen to a member of the Royal family. During the last couple of traumatic decades it's been changing colour with the regularity of a set of traffic lights but whether it's down to tricks of that marvellous Orkney light, an algal bloom or a bona fide miracle, I would not like to say.

Secret Delights of the Museum

Scottish museums are wonderful places and, in the past quarter century, despite a terrible lack of financial support, particularly at a local level, they have continued to bring the story of Scotland to life. Gone are the days of the dusty old display cabinets and the varnished atmosphere that made speaking above a whisper seem like some sort of sacrilege. The range of topics which museums examine is simply staggering. My experience tells me, however, that, despite the splendid new presentations, museums can occasionally be just too much for children – too much information, too many impressions to absorb.

From my own childhood I can recall being taken to the Kelvingrove Museum and Art Gallery in Glasgow, currently undergoing a long-term refurbishment which will transform it into one of the finest art galleries in the world. And what do you imagine caught my attention among so many delights – the Egyptian sarcophagus, the huge stuffed elephant, the armour, the ships, the swords, guns and prehistoric skelingtons? Not a bit of it. My joy was to stand, of a Sunday afternoon, and watch the bees coming and going in the glass-sided hive that was connected to the outside world by a tube in the wall. The community of Kelvingrove bees held me entranced.

SECRET DELIGHTS FROM THE COUNTRY'S MUSEUMS

MUSEUM OF EDINBURGH, THE CAPITAL'S HISTORY

Secret Delight – We all know the story of Greyfriars Bobby, the dog who guarded his master's grave in the city centre churchyard for fourteen years. The Museum has his collar and bowl.

INVERNESS MUSEUM, HISTORY OF THE HIGHLANDS

Secret Delight – The Ardross Wolf is a Pictish stone of beautiful simplicity depicting a creature now vanished from the Highlands but threatening to make a comeback. If you look closely, you may see the wolf breathing!

SHETLAND MUSEUM, LERWICK, ASPECTS OF ISLAND LIFE

Secret Delight – When Hugh Sandison of Nesting went to the Greenland whaling in the 1800s he returned with only one leg, having lost the other to frostbite. The wooden leg he wore for the rest of his life is the museum's pride and joy.

MUSEUM OF CHILDHOOD, EDINBURGH, THE WONDERFUL WORLD OF KIDS

Secret Delight – A century-old doll made by a poor London child from an old shoe – a world away from computer games and square eyes.

BROUGHTY CASTLE MUSEUM, BROUGHTY FERRY, LOCAL HISTORY AND SEASHORE LIFE

Secret Delight – A four-inch-high wooden quaich, or drinking cup, made on a lathe powered by a windmill which stood near the museum. It's a masterpiece of precision craftsmanship in light and dark wood.

MUSEUM OF TRANSPORT, GLASGOW, RACING CARS TO STEAM LOCOS

Secret Delight – An entrancing mock-up of a Glasgow street from the 1930s features an old penny that an imaginative curator has glued to the pavement. The quest for the penny and subsequent efforts to pick it up keep the kids amused for hours.

TANKERNESS HOUSE MUSEUM, KIRKWALL, THE LONG, LONG STORY OF ORKNEY

Secret Delight – A brooch in the shape of the RAF crest made from the Perspex windscreen of a Junkers fighter-bomber shot down in Orkney on Christmas Day, 1940.

DAVID LIVINGSTONE CENTRE, BLANTYRE, LIFE OF THE SCOTS MISSIONARY / EXPLORER

Secret Delight – A trepan or surgeon's cylindrical saw for removing part of skull in order to relieve pressure on the brain. Found in Livingstone's medical kit. Sadly, we do not know if the great man ever employed this terrifying piece of engineering.

SCOTTISH FISHERIES MUSEUM, ANSTRUTHER, THE HISTORY OF SCOTTISH FISHING

Secret Delight – A foot-long metal harpoon head which was used in the Greenland whaling and was twisted into a corkscrew shape by one whale's frantic attempts to escape.

The People's Story, Edinburgh, City Life Since the 1700s

Secret Delight – A photograph of nine-year-old Betty Watson from the early years of the twentieth century showing her wearing the Women's Social and Political Union scarf and captioned 'The Youngest Suffragette' – the museum also has the scarf.

The National Museum of Scotland, Edinburgh, the Nation's Treasures

Secret Delight – A book of sacred poetry which was given to Orcadian Arctic explorer John Rae by the daughter of the vanished adventurer Sir John Franklin and which Rae had to defrost nightly in his sleeping bag before turning over the leaves.

Robert Burns Centre, Dumfries, the Life and Times of Scotland's Bard

Secret Delight – The sword that Rabbie used to strap on during his days as an exciseman in the 1790s.

Maritime Museum, Aberdeen, History of Seagoing

Secret Delight – Two elephant tusks trawled up off Shetland at first thought to be from a mammoth but now believed to be part of a cargo of ivory.

Museum of Scottish Lighthouses, Fraserburgh, Lighthouse History

Secret Delight – A parabolic reflector comprised of 360 tiny mirrors and designed, before the French Revolution, by Dundee's Thomas Smith. This piece of cutting-edge technology from the 1790s is now being readapted for car headlights.

Scotland Street Museum of Education, Glasgow, History of Education

Secret Delight – On the external walls of this building, designed by Charles Rennie Mackintosh, you'll find a host of coloured ceramic tiles – grid patterns and individual tiles, the architect's signature and trademark.

The **Nasty Things** They've Said about the Sons and Daughters of Auld Scotia

The Papal Nuncio and James V were the principal guests of the Earl of Atholl when he had a fantasy woodland palace constructed in Perthshire for a banquet in 1529. Although the palace was torched after the festivities, the papal emissary had clearly been impressed. He wrote, 'It was a great marvel that such a thing could be in Scotland, considering that it was named the arse of the world in other countries.'

Samuel Johnson, the writer and James Boswell's famous pal, generally seemed to have a low opinion of Scotland and the Scots but, in a strange twist, five of the six associates who helped him compile the *Dictionary of the English Language* were from north of the Border. Yet, commenting on the Treaty of Union and the tidal wave of Scots heading south thereafter, he suggested, 'It's not so much to be lamented that Old England is lost, as that the Scotch have found it.' On one occasion, being the guest of a Scots hostess in London, Johnson remarked that the stew that had been served was only fit for hogs. 'Then, pray,' said the lady, 'let me help you to a little more!'

Jonathan Swift, the great satirist, who was very familiar with Scotland around the time of Union, reserved his most acerbic comments for the Scottish aristocracy. According to Swift, the Duke of Argyll was 'an ambitious, covetous, cunning Scot . . . [who] has no principle but his own interest and greatness' and the Earl of Sutherland was 'a blundering, rattle-pated, drunken sot'. We are not about to argue with such as Swift, are we?

Jean Froissart, the famous French chronicler, was reckoned by some to be the world's first 'journalist'. In 1385, he questioned the wisdom of sending up to a thousand French knights to Scotland to support raiding campaigns into England since 'in Scotland you will never find a man of worth: they are like savages who wish not to be acquainted with any one.'

Aeneas Sylvius Piccolomini, the future Pope Pius II, declared, 'The men are small in stature, bold and forward in temper; the women fair in complexion, comely and pleasing, but not for their chastity, giving their kisses more readily than Italian women their hands.' He added that the Scots liked nothing better than to hear the English dispraised. He surely misread the signals?

Don Pedro de Ayala, ambassador of Ferdinand and Isabella at the Court of James IV, in 1498, perceptively remarked, 'They spend all of their time in wars and when there is no war they fight with each other.'

Peter Swave of Lubeck, visiting Edinburgh in 1535, was impressed with the hungry Scot, 'They are ignorant of the use of bread; when they are hungry they outstrip a stag in swiftness of foot, overtake it and kill it, and so sustain life; they eat the flesh raw.'

Nicander Nucius of Venice, who was in Scotland in 1545, thought we compared unfavourably with our southern neighbours, saying, 'For the Scotch are a more barbourous people in their manner of living than the English.'

Estienne Perlin, a French clergyman visiting the country in 1551, struck a note of hope: 'There are some savages in some of the counties of Scotland . . . but the country is in a daily state of improvement.'

Geoffrey of Monmouth, the noted English twelfth-century scholar, whose *Historia Regum Britanniae* went out of its way to badmouth the Scots and confirm English overlordship of the Scots and Picts, described them as 'inferior mongrel breeds'. However, we should not despair because accuracy was not Geoff's strongpoint. He happily located Loch Lomond in Morayshire.

Charles Lamb, the English essayist, wrote, in 1821, that he thought the Scot uncompromising and unable to spot the middle ground: 'I have been trying all my life to like Scotchmen, and am obliged to desist from the experiment in despair.'

John Ray, an eminent English naturalist, toured Scotland in 1661. He was particularly unimpressed by Scottish womenfolk as he found them to be 'none of the handsomest'.

Sir Anthony Weldon produced what must be the most jaundiced holiday postcard of Scotland after his 1617 visit. He toured with James VI and described Scotland as wholesome but for the stinking people that inhabit it. Scotsmen, he suggested, were 'blasphemous, lascivious, violent and stupid barbarians' and he likened being chained in marriage to a Scotswoman to being 'tied to a dead carcass and cast into a stinking ditch'. Weldon was dismissed from the royal household when his views became known.

Stupid, Sir Anthony?
You surely don't mean us!!

Sweet, Sweet Music

Glasgow folk singer Matt McGinn said, in 1969, that, while held in custody for eight hours charged with a national insurance offence, he wrote a song called 'John and Tapi-Yoko' about John Lennon and his wife. Matt, duly chastened after his court appearance, declared, 'I have given some bad performances in my life but this was the worst.'

The Complaining Scot

After much undercover work in the vaults of local authorities through Scotland, I can now unveil the favourite bizarre extracts from letters received by councils and factors over the years. If one these happens to be yours, then step forward and take a bow.

THIS IS TO LET YOU KNOW THAT OOR LAVVIE SEAT IS BROKEN AND WE CANNOT GET BBC2

WILL YOU PLEASE SEND A MAN TAE LOOK AT MY WATER, IT'S MINGIN' AND NOT FIT TO DRINK

OUR KITCHEN FLOOR IS VERY DAMP. WE HAVE TWO WEANS AND WOULD LIKE A THIRD, SO WILL YOU PLEASE SEND SOMEONE TO DO SOMETHING ABOUT IT

WILL YOU PLEASE SEND SOMEONE TO MEND OUR BROKEN PATH? THE WIFE TRIPPED ON IT YESTERDAY AND IS NOW PREGNANT

THE BLOKE NEXT DOOR HAS A LARGE ERECTION IN HIS BACK GARDEN WHICH IS UNSIGHTLY AND DANGEROUS

THE LAVVIE IS BLOCKED AND WE CAN'T BATH THE KIDS UNTIL IT'S CLEARED

THIS NOTE IS JUST TO LET YOU KNOW THAT THERE IS A SMELL COMING FROM THE MAN NEXT DOOR

MY TOILET SEAT IS CRACKED – WHERE DO I STAND?

I REQUEST YOUR PERMISSION TO REMOVE MY DRAWERS IN THE KITCHEN

OUR LAVATORY SEAT HAS BROKEN IN HALF AND IS NOW IN THREE PIECES

Step Forward Olaf of the Sandals

Let's face it, the Vikings still get a bad press despite umpteen documentaries showing how they were worthy settlers, peaceful farmers and general good guys. Somebody is clearly trying to rehabilitate the Norsemen but the truth – unpalatable and politically incorrect as it might be – is that they put themselves about a bit and were not averse to a bit of rape, pillage and even the destruction of the occasional monastery.

That's why the Up-Helly-A' festival in Shetland is so much fun. There's nothing half-hearted, wishy-washy or apologetic about this event which is reckoned to be the biggest fire festival in the world. It's a glorious pagan party that recognises the strong influence of Norse tradition, culture and language in the North of Scotland. Up-Helly-A' unquestionably reflects one of the important strands that make up our multifaceted sense of national identity.

For me, the most intriguing aspect is the way in which the top Viking for the year – the Guizer Jarl – takes on the scary persona of some great Norse warrior or villain for the day to lead the festivities. Here's a sample of names some of the more recent Jarls adopted for their alter egos:

2003: ALEX JOHNSON (OLAF OF THE SANDALS)
1998: COLIN SUMMERS (THORBJORN OF WAST BURRAFIRT)
1994: CHARLES GRANT (GOTURM THE DANE)
1989: WILLIE BLACK (HALFDAN OF BROUSTER)
1984: PETER MALCOLMSON (EIRIK BLOODAXE HARALDSON)
1982: KENNETH CROSSAN (HAKON'S FAKKELBAERE)
1973: ROBERT GEDDES (FLOKI OF THE RAVENS)
1971: ALLAN ANDERSON (TORE THE HOUND)
1965: THOMAS MONCRIEFF (OTTAR THE EXPLORER)

You really wouldn't want to meet that lot on a dark night!

Up-Helly-A' Insights

The fire festival takes place annually on the last Tuesday of January and is said to mark the end of the Yule season. It has become a popular target for international tourists and travel writers. After a torchlight procession of up to a thousand 'guizers', a full-size replica longship, which has been dragged through the streets, is ceremoniously burned. The burning is followed by a night of excessive partying that anthropologists say is very much in the style of the Old Norse celebrations.

During the earlier part of this day packed with activity, the Guizer Jarl and his squad traditionally visit schools, hospitals and eventide homes. It is very much a community day.

THE LONGSHIP CAN TAKE UP TO FOUR MONTHS TO BUILD AND MUCH CARE OVER AS MANY MONTHS IS LAVISHED ON THE COSTUMES.

NOBODY SAYS ANYTHING OFFICIAL BUT A BEARD, THE BUSHIER THE BETTER, IS A 'MUST' FOR ANY GUIZER WORTH HIS SALT.

THE MODERN VERSION OF THE FESTIVAL IS SAID BY SOME TO HAVE BEEN INTRODUCED BY SOLDIERS RETURNING FROM THE NAPOLEONIC WARS AFTER 1815. OTHERS SAY THAT'S A LOAD OF HOOEY!!

TRADITIONAL GEAR FOR 'GUIZERS' MUST INCLUDE WINGED HELMETS, NATTY ARMOUR PLATING, SHEEPSKINS AND THE OBLIGATORY AXE AND SHIELD.

OTHER BURNINGS TAKE PLACE AROUND THIS TIME IN THE SHETLAND COMMUNITIES OF SCALLOWAY, CULLIVOE AND BRAE.

YOU DON'T HAVE TO LOOK FAR TO FIND EVIDENCE THAT THIS IS NOT AN EVENT FOR PANSIES (OR SHRINKING VIOLETS). THE OFFICIAL PROGRAMME STATES DEFIANTLY THAT '**THERE WILL BE NO POSTPONEMENT FOR WEATHER!!!**'.

Culloden — at Last, the Good News!

God forfend that you would ever penetrate my inner sanctum but, should you succeed, you will find, in the corner of my wordsmith's attic, a dusty pile of accounts of the Battle of Culloden. I seldom consult them because the story of the battle is etched in my imagination and the reports fill me with a strange mix of towering rage and black melancholy. The image of the ragged, tired and hungry Highlanders throwing them-selves at the government riflemen, racing misty-eyed across the heather, through the smoke of battle and into history, has always haunted me. The scene makes me mad and sad at the same time.

I always strove to find an anecdote that would lift the gloom, even a little, and, eventually, I came across the remarkable story of Alexander MacIntosh of Essech. Credit for unearthing this marvellous tale, mind you, must go to Robert Forbes, Bishop of Caithness who, in the years after Culloden, made it his cause to harvest stories from the Highlanders who had survived the battle. During a visit to Inverness, Forbes found six candidates for confirmation, including Big Eck, who had a remarkable tale to tell.

At Culloden, MacIntosh had received more than twenty wounds but one of these was literally a lifesaving injury. He was struck down on the battlefield and, as the guns fell silent, was reckoned amongst the clan dead. That he was assumed to be dead is hardly surprising – he was able to show the bishop a criss-cross of scars on his head and face and he had a long scar on the elbow of his right arm. This was the result of a sword blow which had left him able to write but permanently unable to lift his arm above his head.

The Highlander recalled the dragoons arriving 'pall-mall upon my head'. He had no other way to save himself but by throwing his right arm over his head which was the very moment he received the disabling wound. He fell bleeding and unconscious in the heather. After the stripping of the dead had been completed, a party of horsemen and soldiers with fixed bayonets came over the battlefield and, as they approached him, Alex regained consciousness. He could hear the redcoats chatting as they neared him. Alex heard one of them, who was standing above him, say, 'Let's try if this dog be quite dead.' At that, one of the soldiers thrust a bayonet into Alex's buttock.

He told the bishop, 'I happily received the blow without any shrinking or emotion as I had resolved beforehand to endure, if possible, any shock which they might put upon me without shewing (sic) any sign of life. They moved off, declaring me dead enough.' Under cover of darkness the clansman was able to crawl from the battlefield. According to the bishop in a footnote, MacIntosh was a giant of a man in seemingly excellent health. 'I was much taken with him,' added the bishop. And who wouldn't be?

Our Stickiest Export

When, in the Victorian era, Gavan Duffy, director of the Library of Ireland, spoke of the decline of Irish national genius compared to what was going on in Scotland, he chose a rather off-the-wall or, more accurately, in-the-jar comparison. He declared that 'whenever I met, in France, Italy and Egypt, the marmalade manufactured in Dundee, I felt it as a silent reproach.'

They're Human After A'?

After an absence of nearly three hundred years, the Scottish Parliament is now firmly established again but that is not to say there haven't been teething problems. They were to be expected. But, despite the occasional petty squabbles and the righteous public indignation over the cost of the new building (What was wrong with the Royal High School site that a few million wouldn't have fixed?), there is still a great sense of living through a historic period in our nation's story.

To reassure the Scottish public that the party leaders are still locked into day-to-day reality and have not lost a sense of proportion about things that truly matter, I asked them to complete the following wee questionnaire which I hope you'll find enlightening.

Jack McConnell, First Minister (JM)
Jim Wallace, Deputy First Minister (JW)
David McLetchie, Scottish Conservative Party leader (DM)
John Swinney, Scottish National Party leader (JS)
Robin Harper, Scottish Green Party leader (RH)
Tommy Sheridan, Scottish Socialist Party leader (TS)

Question: Which historical figure do you most admire and why?

JM: Those who gave their lives for the freedoms enjoyed by others.

JW: William Wallace.

DM: Winston Churchill.

JS: William Wallace – he established the primacy of freedom for Scots.

RH: Admiral Thomas Cochrane – Cochrane was active at the same time as Nelson. The difference between them was that Nelson was careless of his own life as well as the lives of his men whereas Cochrane fought many successful actions with very little loss of life. Nelson propped up a corrupt monarchy in Naples but Cochrane fought to free Chile from Spanish oppression. He was probably the best tactician in naval history.

TS: John Maclean – he was the greatest socialist leader of the early part of last century.

Question: Nessie – monster or myth?

JM: A monster of a myth.

JW: I believe there is some natural phenomenon there.

DM: Myth.

JS: The fact that that question is still being asked shows the beauty of the Nessie story. It's the mystery that makes the tale special and I like to think of it as just that – a mystery.

RH: Who cares? Nessie is great for tourism. The more myths the better.

TS: Myth.

Question: Who is your favourite public speaker?

JM: I have never heard Nelson Mandela make a speech, but he is the person who has made the biggest impact on my values – his diplomacy, tolerance and ability to forgive makes him a powerful inspiration for us all.

And who can forget Donald Dewar's short, but very powerful, speech at the official opening of the Scottish Parliament on July 1, 1999. He struck completely the right note and made probably the best speech of his life.

JW: Jo Grimond.

DM: George McNeill, the former World Sprint Champion and a marvellous after-dinner raconteur.

JS: Tony Benn for his captivating parliamentary speeches.

RH: George Monbiot, writer and environmentalist.

TS: Tony Benn.

Question: What's your preferred mode of public transport?

JM: The ferry across to Arran, where I grew up. It is a very special place – like Scotland in miniature. I try to get back as often as possible to see my parents. Journeys across the sea are always special for an islander.

JW: Ferries.

DM: Train, especially travelling on the GNER Edinburgh to London route.

JS: My favourite mode of transport is cycling through the peaceful Perthshire countryside at home. As for public transport, during the 2003 election campaign, I crossed the country by train – an eventful experience.

RH: Train. I get a lot of work done on trains and you can get up and walk about. Apart from walking, this is by far and away the best form of transport.

TS: Train.

Question: Your preference – Americans or Europeans?

JM: Both Europe and America contain a rich variety of diverse peoples, despite their common identity. Scotland has a special relationship with both the United States and Europe and as First Minister I am determined to develop those links.

Scotland has a long history of internationalism and achievement – there are Scots and people of Scots ancestry in countries across the world.

Our country has a special place in the hearts and minds of millions around the world – and we will continue to strengthen our cultural, economic and political exchanges on the European and international stage.

JW: Fairly equal as they have very different outlooks.

DM: Americans.

JS: I judge people by who they are not which country or continent they come from.

RH: I have no preference. I have met some perfectly ghastly

Americans, Spanish and Germans – not to mention some irritating Greeks. I've also met likeable people from every country in Europe – many from Spain.

TS: Neither – I am an internationalist.

Question: What do you consider to be the most undesirable trait in people?

JM: Rudeness, and aggression.

JW: Selfishness.

DM: Greed.

JS: Disregard for others.

RH: People who chew gum in the street.

TS: Racism.

Question: Are there any circumstances under which a politician can lie?

JM: Politicians are no different from other people. They should endeavour to be honest and open in all their dealings.

JW: Only in defence of national security.

DM: No — but economy with the truth is not necessary a sin in certain circumstances.

JS: None.

RH: Some people would say that politics is the art of lying without being caught. I prefer to tell the truth.

TS: No.

Question: Who do you think is the most notable Scotswoman?

JM: There are so many, from the past and present. Elsie Inglis whose tireless work to improve maternity facilities was truly ahead of its time, Evelyn Glennie, who has over come disability to be the best in her field, and Margaret Anne Brown, my sister-in-law. She represents all that is great about Scottish women. She cares for her son Paul, who has multiple disabilities, with grace and a can-do attitude that is truly inspirational.

JW: Mary Slessor.

DM: Queen Elizabeth, the Queen Mother.

JS: Mary Slessor – a woman of vision with an international outlook.

RH: Professor Joan Stringer, presently Principal of Napier University. There are still not enough female academics but her career is a shining example to those who would follow in her footsteps.

TS: My mother, Alice.

Question: Which is most important in your opinion — health, wealth or wisdom?

JM: It has to be wisdom. A wise person knows what they have to do to be healthy and stay healthy. And if the opportunities are there, a wise person will always have a good chance to look after their wealth too. But a truly wise person will know that it is the health of our communities and the wealth of talent we have as a country as a whole that will make the biggest contribution to our well being.

JW: Definitely wisdom.

DM: Wisdom.

JS: Health – with wisdom a very close rival.

RH: As party spokesperson on education, I'm tempted to say that wisdom is most important and certainly, in political terms, it's more important to be wise than healthy or wealthy. In ultimate terms, bereft of responsibilities, I would be prepared to swap a considerable quantity of wealth and wisdom for ongoing good health.

TS: Health.

Question: What makes Scotland special?

JM: I love my country. We have some of the world's most

amazing scenery on our doorstep.

Our cultural life is rich and varied – I particularly think this is a very exciting time for our young musicians and singers.

And we should be very proud of our international reputation in 21st century industries such as bio-sciences, electronics and financial services.

But I believe that Scots make Scotland special. We have a great education system, a fantastic reputation and environment and we are amongst the warmest and most hospitable people in the world. As a country, and as Scots, we have every reason to be excited and ambitious about the future, but we do need develop more confidence and belief in ourselves.

JW: The resourcefulness of the people.

DM: The talents and achievements of our people.

JS: Scotland is special because we are a nation with equally strong values of justice and fairness at home and abroad. The passionate desire in Scottish society to create social justice at home is mirrored by a desire to secure fairness throughout the world. Those values have meant that, throughout the centuries, Scots have made a huge contribution overseas. In this uncertain world, I believe our belief in justice, peace and respect for all humanity is more important than ever and I look forward to the day when we can play our full part in delivering these values at home and in promoting these values on the international stage.

RH: Awful winters like long, cold, dark tunnels. Beautiful long summer nights with that very special evening light. The morning light of the Orkneys in the North of Scotland. The dry sense of humour. Good finnan haddie. Aberdeen butteries. Caledonian 80 Shilling. Golspie on a Sunday afternoon.

TS: Its people.

Margaritifera Margaritifera, Wherefore Art Thou?

The unlikely looking freshwater mussel, *Margaritifera margaretifera*, was once the source of Scotland's greatest export – the pearl. The Roman chronicler Suetonius recorded Scottish pearls in the first and second century AD. Interestingly, he suggested that it was the lure of the pearl that prompted Julius Caesar's invasion of Britain. At this time, pearls played an important role in the Roman financial system and the pearls from Scottish rivers were so large that Caesar 'would weigh them in the palm of his hand to judge their value'.

In medieval Scotland, Caledonian pearls ranged alongside the more mundane exports such as fish, leather and wool and were highly sought after in the royal circles of Europe. Necklaces of Scottish pearls were commonly distributed as gifts among Scandinavian aristocracy and were prized for decorating pillows on which the dead rested their heads. One such pillow was found in the Earl of Bothwell's coffin in Denmark.

Scots pearls were treasured at home as well as abroad. Jewels represented wealth in a portable and enduring form at a time when coins and bullion were rare. In 1120, an English church dignitary wrote to the Bishop of St Andrews to request a consignment of pearls 'even if he has to ask the king (Alexander I) who has more than any king'.

James IV had many pearls 'amang his jowalis', including ornate toothpicks and earpicks. The famed jewellery collection of Mary, Queen of Scots is said to have featured a large collection of pearls. The largest pearl, found in an Aberdeenshire river in 1621 and known as the Kellie Pearl, now adorns the Scottish crown jewels. In response to the popularity and utility of pearls, the Privy Council commissioned three gentlemen bailiffs to protect the rivers, control the fishermen and give 'undoubted right' of the pearls found to the King.

Fishing was only allowed in July and August and anyone found to be fishing 'unlaughfully' had their pearls confiscated and were locked in the stocks. Throughout the 1600s, the vogue for the pearl gradually diminished but it was revived again in the 1860s when, in 1865, the pearl produce of Scottish rivers amounted to £12,000.

According to sparse records, it appears that pearl fishing has changed little since Roman times. One method, probably more successful when mussels were abundant in the shallow river beds, required the fisherman to wade through the river, feeling for mussels with his feet and picking them up as they were found. In the Middle Ages, the mussel extraction technique was improved by slipping a slim wooden stick between the gaping valves as the mussels fed. This method was much improved by the use of a glass-bottomed viewer and this technique remains unchanged today. Experts in pearl mussel fishing can select a likely looking specimen and, using specially adapted tongs, open the mussel and remove any pearl, before replacing the mussel on the river bed unharmed. An early record of the practice of pearl fishing was given by Henry Adamson in his poem 'The Muses' Threnodie: or Mirthful Mournings on the Death of Master Gall' (1638).

> *Our shirt-sleeves wreathing up, without more speeches,*
> *And high above our knees we pulling our breeches,*
> *In waters go, then straight mine arms I reach*
> *Unto the ground, whence cleverly I fetch*
> *Some of these living pearled shells, which do*
> *Excell in touching and in tasteing too*
> *As all who search, do by experience try,*
> *And we oftimes; therewith a loudlie cry.*
> *Good Master Gall, behold I found a pearl,*
> *A jewel I assure you for an Earle.*
> *Be silent, said good Gall, or speak at leisure,*
> *For men will cut your throat to get your treasure.*

More Pearls of Wisdom . . .

Until the early twentieth century, a decent living could be made from freshwater pearl fishing. The motor car and access to the countryside changed all that. Now the mussels are at risk of complete extinction and the locations where they do survive are kept a closely guarded secret.

Only a handful of Scottish rivers now contain a viable population of the species whereas there were 160 such rivers just a century ago. However, we do have 60 per cent of the world's remaining population.

Freshwater pearl mussels can live to be 100 but don't become sexually active until their mid teens.

The earliest stage of a mussel's life is spent on the gills of a host fish. In Scotland, they are most commonly found on the gills of salmon and trout.

Of the 250 million fertilised eggs released by a female mussel in her lifetime, only two will survive to adulthood. According to the family mathematician, the mussels have a nine times better chance of winning the national lottery than they have of bringing two of their legions of offspring to maturity.

Mussels containing a pearl are the exception rather than the rule – the pearl forms around small invading parasites.

In cold Scottish rivers, growth rate is very slow, often taking decades.

In the face of pollution, illegal fishing and climate change, the odds are stacked against the species.

Filtering up to 50 litres of water per day, acting as an indicator of water quality and providing a vital link in the freshwater community of Scotland, we should be conserving the mussel for the future whilst recalling its exotic past.

Killiecrankiedotes

- Around the time of the Jacobite victory at the Battle of Killiecrankie in July 1689, Highlanders held a strange belief that cavalry horses underwent special secret training to teach them how to bite enemy infantry and kick out with their hooves in battle.

- *Sir Ewen Cameron of Lochiel, who fought in the battle with the Jacobites, is said to have killed an English officer during the action by biting out his throat.*

- Killiecrankie was the first battle in Europe in which the newly-developed bayonet was employed.

- *Superstitious Highlanders believed that the death of 'Bonnie Dundee', John Graham of Claverhouse, at the battle was down to the fact that he had chosen to wear a green outfit for the battle – green, as you all know, of course, being the secret colour of the fairy people. And, then again, it might have been that random musket shot that caught Claverhouse in the armpit as he rode full tilt into the government lines at the head of his wild Highlanders.*

- Killiecrankie was one of those Scottish battles which, if you'd blinked, you'd have missed it. Best estimates suggest it lasted all of fifteen minutes around 7 p.m. after the armies had faced each other up all day.

Getting To Know Your Favourite Newsreader

JOHN MACKAY (STV)

Home	Glasgow
Status	Married
Favourite holiday destination	North America
Favourite TV programme	*Cheers*
Favourite newsreader	Peter Jennings (ABC News)
Preferred arm-wrestling opponent	Sophie Marceau

GAIL PIRIE (BBC SCOTLAND)

Home	Dingwall
Status	Married
Favourite holiday destination	Miami
Favourite TV programme	*Animal Farm* with the wonderful Ben Fogle
Favourite newsreader	Sir Trevor MacDonald (ITV)
Preferred arm-wrestling opponent	Ben Fogle, of course – he's such a gentleman, he'd surely let me win

FIONA ARMSTRONG (BORDER TV)

Home	Borders
Status	Partnered
Favourite holiday destination	Anywhere with a river and fishing
Favourite TV programme	*Cold Feet*
Favourite newsreader	Sir Trevor MacDonald (ITV)
Preferred arm-wrestling opponent	Jeremy Paxman – he'd stand no chance with an Armstrong!

STEPHEN JARDINE (STV)

Home	Dumfries
Status	Married
Favourite holiday destination	Miami
Favourite TV programme	*Seinfeld*
Favourite newsreader	Dan Rather (CBS)
Preferred arm-wrestling opponent	Margaret Thatcher

LOUISE WHITE (STV)

Home	Glasgow
Status	Married
Favourite holiday destination	Duck, North Carolina
Favourite TV programme	*The West Wing*
Favourite newsreader	Charlotte Green (BBC Radio 4)
Preferred arm-wrestling opponent	James Nesbitt (*Cold Feet*)

DAVID ROBERTSON (BBC SCOTLAND)

Home	Dundee
Status	Married with two sons
Favourite holiday destination	India, no – Australia, no – New Mexico – um, the questions have been easy up until now!
Favourite TV programme	*Angel* (*Buffy the Vampire Slayer* spin-off)
Favourite newsreader	Does Alan Partridge count?
Preferred arm-wrestling candidate	A man with both arms in a sling!

SARAH HEANEY (STV)

Home	Dublin
Status	Partnered
Favourite holiday destination	Mallorca or the Côte d'Azur
Favourite TV programme	*Sex and the City*
Favourite Newsreader	Nicholas Owen (ITV)
Preferred arm-wrestling opponent	Nicholas Cage

PENNY MACMILLAN (BBC)

Home	Galashiels
Status	Married
Favourite holiday destination	Any tropical island or a good ski resort.
Favourite TV programme	*The Holiday Programme*
Favourite newsreader	Anna Ford (BBC)
Preferred arm-wrestling candidate	My husband

Keeping it Tight

In this age of single-word book titles, conciseness is every-thing. A few centuries back, however, publishers and authors were not so picky. If you could tell half the story in the title, then so much the better. In the aftermath of the 1745 Jacobite uprising, adventure stories of the Prince's 'doings' among the heather were the business. One book on this theme revelled in the title of *Ascanius, or the Young Adventurer, containing a particular account of all that happened to a certain person during his wanderings in the North from his memorable defeat in April 1745 to his final escape on the 19th of September in the following year.* According to Scottish historian Tom Devine, this became a best-seller in French, Spanish and Italian. Today, I bet publishers would demand something substantially briefer for a title, such as *Fugitive* or *The Scunnered Stuart*.

The Definitive Scots Palindrome

If, like me, you have trouble spelling words in the orthodox, left-to-right fashion, then the palindrome – a word, phrase or sentence that has the same sequence of letters read in either direction – is a bit of a black hole. However, this is one worth savouring, I think. Picture the scene. Having been chased by the witches who steal his old mare Meg's tail, Tam o' Shanter and Meg escape and stop to catch their breath. Meg, as she would, suggests that they go back and sort out the hags at Kirk Alloway but Tam responds,

'Revenge Meg, Never!'
'!reveN, geM egneveR'

'The Covenanters' Grace'

Traditionally, these lines are entitled 'The Selkirk Grace' and are attributed to the pen of Robbie Burns. In fact, they were known as 'The Covenanters' Grace' in Galloway long before Burns was a boy:

> *Some hae meat that canna eat,*
> *An' some wad eat that want it,*
> *But we hae meat an' we can eat,*
> *Sae let the Lord be thankit.*

Keys to the Kingdom

One of the most shameful episodes in the Scottish Wars of Independence came in 1296 when Edward I, victor at the Battle of Dunbar, arrived at Stirling to find its defenders had fled, leaving a porter with instructions to hand over the keys to the English invaders. Although Scotland soon moved on to conduct a policy of guerrilla warfare against England in the later Middle Ages, our record in pitched battles is quite impressive. Of the fourteen battles fought between 1297 and 1513, eight resulted in Scottish victories.

The Biggest Scrum in the World – the Kirkwall Ba' Game

Ba' Games are still found in several parts of the United Kingdom but the four Kirkwall Ba' Games, staged every year in Orkney's capital, are the most spectacular of them all. On both Christmas Day and New Year's Day, a men's game and a boys' game take place, sometimes lasting up to seven hours. For over 200 years, the two sides – the Up-the-Gates (Uppies) and the Down-the-Gates (Doonies) – have battled through the streets. Each 'team' – a loose term for what is essentially a steaming mass of humanity – aims to carry, smuggle, run, throw, kick or simply force the handmade leather ba', through sheer weight of numbers, into the goal. In the case of the Uppies, the goal is the site of an old castle opposite the Catholic Church and, for the Doonies, it is the sea – normally within the basin of the harbour. So, around the turn of the year Kirkwall bears all the hallmarks of a town under siege with shop and house windows barricaded with wooden batons and looking eerily like the centre of Pamplona prior to the running of the bulls.

The scrum in the men's game can be over 200-strong and woe betide the onlooker caught up in the melee. Despite this, injuries are seldom serious – even in the heart of the scrum. The rules are a good indication of the intensity of the action and the particular problems onlookers can encounter. They include, for example, the following:

- spectators must not climb on walls or roofs
- children must be kept at a safe distance (particularly those being carried as they are very vulnerable should the game erupt!)
- spectators are asked to give considerable leeway in confined areas as a 'breakaway may create problems'

In addition, the players are warned that there must be no unnecessary violence.

Tradition plays a big part in this street game. A Doonies' win, it's said, will signify good fishing while victory for the Uppies is a portent of a successful potato and barley harvest. A Ba' winner is selected after each event and considerable refreshment is, of course, compulsory. Expatriates come from the world over to join in the ritual but a women's Ba', first staged after World War II, never gained acceptance among the menfolk. Results since 1872 are listed below:

Christmas Day Men's Ba'
DUUUUUDUUUUUUUUUUWWWWWDDU
UUDDUUUDUDDDUDDDUWWWWWDUU
DDDDDUUDUDDUDDUDDDUUUUUUUU
UDUDDDDDDUDDDDDDUUUDDDDUUUUUU

Christmas Day Boy's Ba'
DUUDUDDDDDDDDDDDUDDDWWWWW
DUUDDUDDDDDDDDDDDDUWWWWW
DDUUDDUUUUUDUDUUUUUUDDDUDDD
DDDUUDDDDDUUUUUUDDUUUDUUUDUUU

New Year's Day Men's Ba –
UUDDUUDDDUUDDUUUUUDUUUUUUUUU
UUWWWWWDUDUUDUUUDDDUDDUDDDU
WWWWWUUUUUDDUUDDDUUUUUDDDDDUDDD
UUUDUUUDDDDDUDDDDDDUUUUUDDDDUUUUU

New Year's Day Boy's Ba
UDDDDUUDDDDDDDDDDDUUUWWWWW
UUDUUDUUDUDDDDDDUDUDWWWWWDU
UUUDDUUUUUDUUDDUUDUDUDUDDDUD
DUUDDDDUDUUUUUDDDDDUUUUUDDUDU

KEY: U=Uppies D=Doonies W=cancelled due to World War

Anything to Declare?
The Wee Outburst of Arbroath, 6 April 1320

It's been called the definitive exposition of Scottish identity, a clarion call for democracy, the most impressive manifesto of nationalism produced in medieval Europe, the precursor of constitutional monarchy in Scotland.

And, in addition, the Declaration of Arbroath was a right cheeky piece of work in which the nobility threatened to turf the king out if he misbehaved. The 'hundred of us' section is the acid test of true Scottishness. If you can read this aloud without a lump in your sporran or a tear in your eye then your Caledonian roots must be questioned.

There is no doubt that the Declaration of 1320, a letter sent by the Scottish barons to Pope John XXII, was an important document but, basically, it was a diplomatic response to English assertions of overlordship that were under consideration by the Pope. For nearly 400 years, the Declaration was a lost national treasure. It did not surface again until the late 1600s when it was used by those arguing against the divine right of kings. Here are the core elements in this remarkable document:

The Signature bit

The following is a list of those who put their names to the Declaration. They addressed their letter to 'the most Holy Father and Lord in Christ, the Lord John, by divine providence Supreme Pontiff of the Holy Roman and Universal Church, his humble and devout sons':

Duncan, Earl of Fife,
Thomas Randolph, Earl of Moray,
Lord of Man and of Annandale,
Patrick Dunbar, Earl of March,
Malise, Earl of Strathearn,
Malcolm, Earl of Lennox,
William, Earl of Ross,
Magnus, Earl of Caithness
and Orkney,
William, Earl of Sutherland:
Walter, Steuart of Scotland,
William Soules, Butler of Scotland,
James, Lord of Douglas,
Roger Moubray,
David, Lord of Brechin,
David Graham,
Ingram Umfraville,
John Menteith, guardian of the
earldom of Menteith,
Alexander Fraser,
Gilbert Hay, Constable of Scotland,
Robert Keith, Marischal of Scotland,
Henry St Clair,
John Graham.

David Lindsay,
William Oliphant,
Patrick Graham,
John Fenton,
William Abernethy,
David Wemyss,
William Mushet,
Fergus of Ardrossan,
Eustace Maxwell,
William Ramsay,
William Mowat,
Alan Murray,
Donald Campbell,
John Cameron,
Reginald Cheyne,
Alexander Seton,
Andrew Leslie,
Alexander Straiton,
Alexander Lamberton,
Eduard Keith,
John Inchmartin,
Thomas Mengies,
John Durrant,
Thomas Morham

Found your family name among that lot? If not and you're still desperate to have some connection with this unique piece of history, then don't despair. Attached to the Declaration is one more name and – sadly, or maybe not so sadly – it is totally illegible. This gives every Scot the tantalising yet cheering possibility that their family name may be on the declaration. If you look at closely at it under a light, surely that could be your surname – Simeone, Jorgensen, Wu, Khan, even Hewitson. After all, scratch a Scot these days and you'll find us all underneath.

The cheeky bit

'Yet if he (King Robert Bruce) should give up what he has begun, and agree to make us or our kingdom subject to the King of England or the English, we should exert ourselves at once to drive him out as our enemy and a subverter of his own rights and ours, and make some other man who was well able to defend us our King.'

The best bit

'For, as long as but a hundred of us remain alive, never will we on any condition be brought under English rule. It is in truth not for glory, nor riches, nor honour that we are fighting, but for freedom – for that alone, which no honest man gives up but with life itself.'

C'mon you Scots!!!

No Way is the King Quair!

James I, King of Scots, wrote a work called 'The Kingis Quair' ('The King's Work'), a long poem in Scots in which he showed himself to be a bit of a ladies' man – as these few stanzas indicate:

> And therewith cast I doun mine eyes again,
> Whereat I saw walking under the tower,
> Full secretly, now comen here to plain
> The fairest or the freshest younge flower
> That e'er I saw methought, before that hour:
> For which sudden abate, anon astart
> The blood of all my body to my heart
>
> And though I stood abasit for a lite,
> No wonder was; for why? My wittis all
> Were so o'ercome with pleasance and delight –
> Only through letting of my eyen fall –
> That suddenly my heart became her thrall
> For ever of free will, for of menace
> There was no token in her sweet face.

The target of his affection was Henry V's cousin, Lady Jane Beaufort, whom he married in 1424. I think this most definitely confirms that the kingis in no ways quair!

Talent Spotting not his Forte

One of the trustees of Edinburgh Academy, who prided himself on his ability to identify people with artistic skills, was George Thomson. In one young man, he failed to see any merit, saying that he was 'incapable of receiving instruction even in the most ordinary branches of his art'. This young man was Robert Burns.

John Barbour's View of Freedom

Ah! Freedom is a noble thing!
Freedom makes man to have liking!
Freedom and solace to man gives:
He lives at ease that freely lives!
A noble heart may have none ease
Nor ellys nought that may him please,
If freedom fail: for free liking
Is yearned o'er all other thing,
Nor he, that aye has lived free
May not well know the property,
The anger, nor the wretched doom
That is coupled to foul thraldom,
But, if he had essayed it,
Then all perquer he should it wit;
And should think freedom more to prize
Than all the gold in world that is.

John Barbour (1320–95)

By the Way, It's Worth Noting That

Life is mostly froth and bubble
Two things stand like stone,
KINDNESS in another's trouble,
COURAGE in your own.

Adam Lindsay Gordon (1833–70)

If You Can't Stand the Heat — Get Oot o' the Smiddy!

Names are simply handles, aren't they? – just a way of identifying us within the flock of humanity. They don't reach in and tell you about the soul of an individual. For example, one of the roughest, most obnoxious people I have ever encountered was a man called Gentles.

Parents don't make it easy. What were Mr and Mrs Long thinking about when they named their firstborn Miles? Yes, it happened. That man with the telling phrase for every moment, Sam Goldwyn, once asked a couple of proud new parents why they had called their baby John. Said Sam, 'Every Tom, Dick and Harry is called John.'

The 2001 survey of surnames, organised by the General Registry Office for Scotland, proved a goldmine of information for name enthusiasts. The most remarkable phenomenon is surely the continuing and ubiquitous presence of the 'Smiths'. I have read many times of how many horses we Scots had in centuries past but if we look at the league tables of most commonly found names you get the feeling there must have been a blacksmith for every cuddy. Or perhaps labouring daily in close proximity to the fiery forge pushed up the Smithsonian sperm count.

In Scotland the most recent survey found that Smith is the most common in twenty out of thirty-two areas, with their dominance most noted in the cities. Smith came second in four of the other areas. Interestingly, there was only one area where it didn't appear in the top ten and that was Orkney. This seems to suggest that Orkney has been less touched by outside influence than other parts of Scotland. Below you'll find the top ten most popular names in 2001 in each administrative district with a note of the most popular name a century previously in the roughly equivalent administrative area, where available:

TOP TEN SCOTTISH NAMES

Aberdeen City
2001 Smith, Duncan, Reid, Stewart, Robertson, Milne, Thomson, Davidson, Taylor, Fraser
1901 Smith

Aberdeenshire
2001 Smith, Thomson, Buchan, Anderson, Reid, Duncan, Wilson, Taylor, Milne, Robertson

Angus
2001 Smith, Stewart, Robertson, Brown, Anderson, Milne, Clark, Mitchell, Duncan, Thomson
1901 Smith

Argyll and Bute
2001 Campbell, Macdonald, Smith, Brown, Cameron, Stewart, Maclean, Wilson, Scott, Robertson
1901 Campbell

Clackmannanshire
2001 Hunter, Thomson, Wilson, Paterson, Anderson, Smith, Robertson, Brown, Stewart, Taylor, McEwan
1901 Hunter

Dumfries and Galloway
2001 Smith, Wilson, Thomson, Graham, Bell, Brown, Johnstone, Little, Campbell, Anderson
1901 Bell

Dundee City
2001 Smith, Stewart, Robertson, Mitchell, Anderson, Thomson, Brown, Taylor, Duncan, Wilson
1901 Smith

East Ayrshire
2001 Wilson, Smith, Brown, Campbell, Murray, Stewart, Clark, Young, Wallace, Kerr, Johnstone
1901 Wilson

East Dunbartonshire
2001 Smith, Campbell, Brown, Thomson, Wilson, Stewart,
    Robertson, Macdonald, Scott, McDonald
1901 Campbell

East Lothian
2001 Smith, Thomson, Brown, Scott Wilson, Stewart,
    Robertson, Reid, Anderson, Young
1901 Thomson

East Renfrewshire
2001 Smith, Miller, Wilson, Stewart, Brown. Campbell,
    Anderson, Young, Robertson, Reid
1901 Campbell

Edinburgh City
2001 Smith, Robertson, Anderson, Brown, Wilson,
    Thomson, Scott, Stewart, Campbell, Young
1901 Brown

Eilean Siar (Western Isles)
2001 Macleod, Macdonald, Morrison, Mackenzie, Mackay,
    Campbell, Maclean, Maciver, Murray, Smith

Falkirk
2001 Smith, Wilson, Brown, Robertson, Anderson,
    Thomson, Campbell, Stewart, Marshall, Bell

Fife
2001 Smith, Wilson, Brown, Thomson, Robertson,
    Anderson, Stewart, Campbell, Paterson, Taylor, Scott
1901 Thomson

Glasgow
2001 Smith, Campbell, Brown, Stewart, Wilson, Thomson,
    Kelly, Robertson, Murray, Anderson
1901 Smith

Highland

2001 Macdonald, Mackenzie, Mackay, Ross, Macleod,
Fraser, Campbell, Sutherland, Smith, Stewart
1901 McDonald

Inverclyde

2001 Campbell, Smith, Wilson, Anderson, Docherty,
Stewart, Brown, Kelly, Thomson, Robertson, Mitchell,
Cameron
1901 Campbell

Midlothian

2001 Smith, Thomson, Robertson, Wilson, Watson, Brown,
Anderson, Stewart, Campbell, Scott
1901 Brown

Moray

2001 Smith, Stewart, Morrison, Grant, Duncan, Campbell,
Fraser, Reid, Anderson, Murray
1901 Fraser

North Ayrshire

2001 Smith, Wilson, Brown, Campbell, Thomson, Reid,
Stewart, Kerr, Ferguson, Anderson
1901 Wilson

North Lanarkshire

2001 Smith, Brown, Campbell, Wilson, Stewart, Thomson,
Hamilton, Anderson, Robertson, Miller
1901 Smith

Orkney Islands

2001 Rendall, Drever, Sinclair, Flett, Scott, Tait, Craigie,
Muir, Harcus, Spence
1901 Sinclair

Perth and Kinross

2001 Stewart, Robertson, Smith, Brown, Thomson,
Anderson, Scott, Reid, Taylo,r Macdonald
1901 Robertson

Renfrewshire
2001 Smith, Campbell, Wilson, Brown, Stewart, Kerr, Kelly,
Anderson, Robertson, Thomson / Reid
1901 Campbell

Scottish Borders
2001 Scott, Brown, Wilson, Smith, Young, Thomson,
Turnbull, Anderson, Douglas, Bell
1901 Scott

Shetland Islands
2001 Johnson, Smith, Williamson, Jamieson, Robertson,
Anderson, Leask, Irvine, Thomson, Manson
1901 Smith

South Ayrshire
2001 Smith, Wilson, Brown, Campbell, Thomson, Kerr,
Clark, Young, Stewart, Murray
1901 Wilson

South Lanarkshire
2001 Smith, Brown, Wilson, Thomson, Campbell, Hamilton,
Stewart, Robertson, Anderson, Murray
1901 Smith

Stirling
2001 Stewart, Campbell, Wilson, Robertson, Brown, Taylor,
Smith, Thomson, Macdonald, Walker, Ross, Morrison
1901 Brown

West Dunbartonshire
2001 Campbell, Smith, Brown, Wilson, Thomson, Stewart,
Murray, Anderson, Hamilton, Gallacher
1901 Campbell

West Lothian
2001 Smith, Brown, Robertson, Wilson, Anderson, Stewart,
Thomson, Campbell, Walker, Scott
1901 Brown

Hallowe'en for Beginners

Hark, the Whirlwind is in the Wood!
A Low Murmur in the Vale!
It is the Mighty Army of the Dead
Returning from the Air!

Macpherson's anglicising of an old Gaelic verse

The end of October is the time of year when all of us should be getting a bit closer to the Celtic side of our nature. Yes, boys and girls, we all have it whether or not we're of the Copland Road persuasion.

It is important to remember also that this is not just a time for children. It is a time of year, marking the entry into winter, the ingathering of the harvest and, perversely for the ancient races, it was the start of the New Year. Yes, it was the Celtic Hogmanay and, if you can think of a better reason for a party, then you're a better man than I am, Finn MacCool.

Samhuinn was the Celtic name for this autumn festival and, just to add to the unbridled fun, it was a day when the dead were welcomed back into the family. Ma, pa and the weans would troop down to the nearest megalithic monument, which often marked the ancient burial grounds, and the fun would begin with the ethereal ancestors flitting around and joining in the activities.

Games, races, general partying, a touch of orgiastic houghmagandy was the order of the day and it was a time when we were all expected to dress up 'gaily' and, God forfend, recite poetry in public! Here are some of the Hallowe'en snippets which I've harvested over the years:

> Transport for witches at Hallowe'en was varied – the ubiquitous broomstick, sieves, eggshells (I remember my granny

smashing eggshells for that very reason on the big day) and tabby cats that were miraculously transformed into coal black steeds for the night.

Hallowe'en was also flitting time for the fairies who often moved on to a new hill. Fairy processions were often encountered.

Tip – if, for some reason best known to yourself, you want to enter a fairy hill, you must walk round it clockwise nine times and a door will be opened unto you. One slight drawback of doing this is that you have to spend the rest of eternity there.

Bonfires were always an important aspect of Hallowe'en with the ashes from the blaze being scattered around to ward off evil spirits and witches. It's said that, in the mid 1800s on Hallowe'en in the Buchan district of Aberdeenshire, up to eighty bonfires could be seen from one point.

Queen Victoria had a special Hallowe'en event at Balmoral – 'The Burning of Shandy Dann'. A huge bonfire was lit in front of the castle and, with the clansmen mustered in their obligatory tartan, the effigy of an old woman was burned to the skirl of the pipes. 'No one entered more heartily into this curious rite than the head of empire herself,' said one observer.

Two pipers were found wandering the streets of Inverness a few years back and their inability to dodge the cars and buses led to them being taken into protective custody by the local constabulary. They were baffled by the way Inverness had changed and it transpired that they had entered the fairy kingdom on Hallowe'en on their way back from the Battle of Sheriffmuir in 1715. Time displacement, urban myth or simply a fairy tale. Who knows?

Scotland's Rattlin' Good Relics

In pre-Reformation days, the Scots army always went to war with a suitable selection of the relics of the saints – bones, mostly – safely stowed in the baggage train. These were believed to bring good fortune although, if you look at the result tables over the years, this was never guaranteed.

Just before Bannockburn, the forearm of St Fillan is said to have lifted the lid of its gold reliquary and waved confidently at Robert Bruce. The patriot king knew that, after this supernatural event, he was on to a winner against the might of England.

The biggest lay success of the fourteenth century in the relic-gathering business belonged to William Preston. In 1455, he gifted the arm of St Giles to his own church of St Giles in Edinburgh after 'acquiring' it on a pilgrimage to the saint's shrine near Marseilles in the south of France.

The number of multiple heads, arms, legs, teeth, eyebrows and even foreskins doing the rounds in Europe in the Middle Ages reached quite staggering proportions. The church was seemingly happy enough to explain that the saints, being very special individuals, could replicate themselves endlessly. This reached a bizarre stage when a dispute arose, between the East Lothian villages of Auldhame, Tynninghame and Preston, as to which community should have the privilege of enshrining the remains of St Baldred. The saint obligingly turned his corpse into three complete bodies, keeping everyone happy.

Scotland's long-dead saints were not averse to putting in a hard shift on behalf of their country when the call came. Two hundred years after his death, Orkney's St Magnus was on triple time as events at Bannockburn unfolded in 1314. A vision of the saint was reported at far-off Glastonbury on the eve of the battle – he apparently indicated that he was just stopping off for a breather on his way to join the Scots line-up. Then he was seen, in shining armour, riding through the streets of Aberdeen and, finally, he was reported sailing across the Pentland Firth to bring the glad news of the great Scottish victory to his native Orkney.

'That Bastard Verdict'

It was Sir Walter Scott, a writer not slow to turn a telling phrase, who so described the unusual three-hundred-year-old Scottish alternative verdict of 'not proven'.

Scottish law is out of step with most of the rest of the so-called civilised world in allowing this third verdict of 'not proven'.

This oddity of Scots law is known to have caused much scratching of venerable American journalistic heads when it was pointed out that this outcome would be available when a Scottish court convened in Holland to try the two men accused of the Lockerbie bombing.

The 'not proven' verdict is very much alive and in regular use in Scottish courts. In recent years, it has formed almost one quarter of the several thousand annual acquittals passed down by Scottish judges and juries (in 2001, 4500 people were acquitted in Scottish courts).

Generally, the proportion of people acquitted receiving a 'not proven' verdict' varies with the type of crime. It is, for example, more common in cases of indecency, unlawful use of a vehicle and serious assault while it is less often returned in alleged offences of shoplifting and vandalism.

Technically, 'not proven' has the same effect as a 'not guilty verdict', namely, that the accused is acquitted and cannot be tried again for the same offence – although this is not the generally perceived public view.

Legal experts, however, suggest the verdict indicates that the jurors felt the accused was guilty but this could not be proved beyond reasonable doubt.

This 'guilty, not guilty' option was introduced to Scotland by Oliver Cromwell during the Commonwealth in the 1650s. Before and after the Commonwealth, Scotland used a 'proven, not proven' system.

The 'not guilty' outcome was added to the Scottish options when, in a historic case, centuries ago, concerning a fatal duel, a jury felt so emphatically that a man was not guilty of a particular offence that they simply spurned the system and found him 'not guilty'.

The most famous 'not proven' verdict in Scottish legal history is generally recognised to have been that of Madeleine Smith, the twenty-two-year-old daughter of an Glasgow architect, who was charged, on three counts, of the murder of her lover. One 'not guilty' verdict and two 'not proven' verdicts were returned.

In recent years, there have been several efforts to have the verdict removed from the statute books but it continues to defy its critics.

In the eyes of the accused, 'not proven' is seen as a 'not guilty' verdict but often, for a victim or their family, it is thought of as a 'guilty' verdict. Much criticism has been levelled at the 'not proven' verdict because of this strange legal anomaly.

Difficulty Factor — Severe

An old Scots saying hints that lawyers may be the cause of the undeserved Scottish reputation for stinginess. It suggests: 'It's as easy to get siller frae a lawyer as butter frae a black dog's throat.' Difficult then?

Kelpie Sightings

Water sprites, in the shape of bulls and horses, were commonly reported in the Scottish Highlands, their favourite haunts being lonely, mist-covered lochs. Sutherland has, over the centuries, been particularly favoured by these spectral farmyard animals. Many, many people thought they had seen them but investigation often proved the sightings to be ordinary animals transformed by the imagination (and perhaps some suitable lubricant) into mythical creatures. Oddly-shaped rocks and the unusual light on the high moors also accounted for many supposed sightings. Having dealt with all of these qualifications, there are, indeed, stories of loch kelpies that do take some explaining.

There are a number of lochs where you are most likely to catch a glimpse of the legendary water horse or bull – Assynt, Arkaig, Shiel, Lochy, Quoich, Canisp, Oich, Morar, Ness, Rannoch, Awe and, a wee bit further south, St Mary's Loch at Yarrow in the Borders, among others.

So prevalent were the stories of the water horses that sporting English gentlemen in Victorian times would organise shooting parties to track down the legendary beast.

Waves on a lochan on a calm day were always blamed on the submarine stomping of the spectral bulls and horses.

Big-eared calves or foals with distended nostrils and a fiery spirit were sure indicators that the water spirit had been a-courting among the mares and cows.

In Shetland these water beasties were known as 'nuggles'.

The water sprite may seem like a friendly creature but it is single-minded in wishing to drag you to the bottom of the loch. Once you have lain hand on the horse or bull it is impossible to let go. One enterprising Highland lad is said to have chopped his hand off at the wrist to avoid descending into the depths.

In the parish of Fearn in Forfarshire, there is said to be a slab of sandstone with the print of a kelpie's hoof impressed in the rock.

The Gaelic name for the fabled water horse is *Each-uisge*.

How Sick Was the Red Comyn?

No one today questions the fact that Robert Bruce had a bloody hand in the despatching of his distant relative John Comyn the Younger in the Church of the Minorite Friars, Dumfries, on 10 February, 1306. We even have a traditional version of the dialogue in the immediate aftermath of the murder as the assassins were out in the churchyard discussing the state of play.

Bruce appeared with the dripping blade in his hand and declared, 'I must be off, for doubt I have slain the Red Comyn.'

'Doubt!' cried Roger Kirkpatrick of Closeburn. 'I'll mak' siccar.'

The authenticity of this exchange is said to be confirmed by the fact that the declaration was adopted, in the late fifteenth century, as the official motto on the arms of the Kirkpatricks.

Personally, I prefer the later, irreverent rendering of the exchange between Bruce and Kirkpatrick which runs:

Bruce: 'I've just left the Red Comyn and he looks unco sick.'
Kirkpatrick: 'I'll mak' him sicker!'

The Clan Donald Weather Stone

The story goes that, during the fourteenth century, a loyal Donald clansman arrived at the court of the Lord of the Isles with a stone, claiming that it was a treasure more mystical than the Holy Grail and more valuable than the Crown jewels. He had obtained this miraculous object during a visit to the Outer Hebrides. The traveller explained that the local Macdonalds were a primitive lot, having no written word and only a primitive knowledge of agriculture. However, the Macdonalds did have a simple yet ingenious method of determining the weather. They suspended this stone on a thong from a tree and used it as Scotland's first barometer or weather indicator.

The secret formula, guarded over generations, for unravelling the complexities and interpreting the messages of the stone can now, for the first time in seven centuries, be revealed.

A DRY STONE MEANS IT IS NOT RAINING

.... A WET STONE MEANS IT IS RAINING

A SHADOW UNDER THE STONE MEANS THE SUN IS SHINING

.... IF YOU CAN'T SEE THE STONE, IT IS DARK

IF THE STONE SWINGS, THEN A STRONG WIND IS BLOWING

.... IF THE STONE IS WHITE ON TOP, IT IS SNOWING

IF THE STONE JUMPS UP AND DOWN, THERE IS AN EARTHQUAKE

.... IF YOU CAN SEE THROUGH THE STONE, THEN IT'S
TIME YOU LAID OFF THE HOME BREW

How Well do you Know your Scottish Banknotes?

In most countries, governments normally issue banknotes through their central banks but, in Scotland, three banks – the Royal Bank of Scotland, the Bank of Scotland and the Clydesdale Bank – issue notes, exercising a privilege that came about in the seventeenth century.

The first bank to do this was the Bank of Scotland which, immediately after opening in 1695, introduced paper currency. The whole idea was viewed initially with suspicion but, once it became clear that the bank could honour its promise to pay, the system grew in popularity and was soon found to be very convenient. Scotland was one of the first countries to use paper currency from choice and the circulation of notes soon increased.

The Royal Bank, founded in 1727, issued notes on its founding.

The first notes were bound in books, like modern cheques but without perforations. They were often cut out with a knife or scissors or, in haste, torn from the stub.

In the 1700s, each twenty shilling note (one pound) was in circulation for about nine months – much the same as today's £1 notes (now themselves a bit of a rarity, with the Royal Bank being the only bank to issue them and then just in small batches).

Early notes were printed in black and it was not until 1777 that the Royal Bank pioneered colour with a blue rectangle and the king's head shown in red.

Banknotes provided a crucial part of Scotland's eighteenth- and early-nineteenth-century currency. It is known that, at times, £1 notes were torn in halves and quarters.

As well as the increasingly complex designs that were employed to fox the forger, banks introduced water-marked paper, signatures and seals, all of which meant that attempting to counterfeit the notes would be a tricky business.

Death or amputation of tongue were common punishments for forging banknotes.

Sir Walter Scott led a successful Scottish campaign in 1826 against an English plan to forbid the circulation of all notes under £5.

Try this wee quiz – without looking in your wallet or purse. Look at the list of descriptions below of the backs of Scottish banknotes and try to match them up with the appropriate denomination. Not as easy as you might imagine. And remember – nae keekin! We are talking here of £1, £5, £10, £20, £50 and £100 denomination notes. As if anyone I know would have a 100-smackeroonie note in their pooch! Oh, yes, a couple of wee clues – The Royal Bank does not produce a £50 note but they are the only bank to produce a £1 note. For the results and your credit rating, see below:

1. .... BANK OF SCOTLAND'S 'SCOTTISH LIFE' SERIES
                   a) Distilling/Brewing
                   b) Arts/Culture
                   c) Tourism
                   d) Oil Industry
                   e) Education/Research

2. .... ROYAL BANK OF SCOTLAND'S 'CASTLES' SERIES
                   a) Balmoral
                   b) Brodick
                   c) Edinburgh
                   d) Culzean
                   e) Glamis

3. .... CLYDESDALE BANK'S 'GREAT SCOTS' SERIES
        a) Mary Slessor
        b) Lord Kelvin
        c) Robert Bruce
        d) Robert Burns
        e) Adam Smith

The three big banks agreed on a uniform colour scheme for notes of the same denomination. Again, without taking a sly peek, try to match the colour to the denomination.

4. .... COLOURS
        a) Blue
        b) Maroon/Purple
        c) Brown
        d) Red
        e) Green (NB: there are two possible answers here)

Answers

1. a) £10; b) £50; c) £100; d) £5; e) £20;

2. a) £100; b £20; c) £1; d) £5; e) £10;

3. a) £10; b £100; c) £20; d) £5; e) £50;

4. a) £5; b) £20; c) £10; d) £100; e) £50 (plus RBS £1)

YOUR RATING OUT OF 20
1–5 correct: you're spending money like it's going out of style so you've got no time to admire designs!
5–15 correct: your bar presence is lacking – too much time pondering your pounds!
15–20 correct: time to count your dosh again, you borderline Scrooge!

A Whole Flights of Stairs

Just occasionally, when mention is made of the Treaty of Union in 1707, the name of John, the 1st Earl of Stair, surfaces. He was an ardent supporter of Union who, when the debate came round to Scottish representation at Westminster, delivered an impassioned speech defending the proposals – then promptly went home and died. Family and supporters put it down to overwork but, of course, the rest of Scotland was convinced it was down to his treachery.

Stair is better known, perhaps, as the Secretary of State who, in 1692, got the blame for permitting the Massacre of Glencoe. Scottish history is filled with bogeymen but some of the Jacobite persuasion would make the case for Stair being 'Villain Number One'. As often happens, the activities of such people become mythologised and, in the 1700s, the mere mention of his name would have set the bairns a-greetin' and the cat screeching up the lum.

As it happens, his story overshadows other Stair family members whose odd stories, I think, deserve to be better known. His father was James Dalrymple, Viscount Stair, an eminent lawyer and statesman. Apparently, in 1641, he had been given a captaincy in the Covenanting army but he was also chasing the post of Chair of Philosophy at the University of Glasgow. In those days, the post was won by competing in debate and James, the bold boy, turned up in his scarlet uniform, complete with sword, for the debate. Did he intimidate the other competitors and the learned professors? Difficult to say but he did get the job. He is probably best remembered as the author of what is still regarded as the most authoritative work on Scots Law – *The Institutions of the Law of Scotland* – which has also come to be regarded as one of the building blocks of the eighteenth-century Enlightenment.

This, of course, was the era of powerful dynasties and political managers such as the Dalrymples and the Dundases. On the trail of the Dalrymples, I came across this smashing wee quatrain, written by Lord Auchinleck. A wimple is a piece of trickery and the verse runs thus:

> *First cam the men o' many wimples,*
> *In Common Language ca'd Da'rumples,*
> *And after them cam the Dundases,*
> *Wha raide oor lords and lairds like asses.*

Not a particularly edifying picture of the independence and integrity of our eighteenth-century landed classes.

John was also the name of the 2nd Earl of Stair who was exiled to Holland after accidentally shooting his elder brother dead at the age of eight. He studied at Leyden – as many other Scots did at that time – becoming a notable military figure, serving as aide-de-camp to Duke of Marlborough and commanding an infantry brigade at the Battle of Ramillies. An ambassador to several countries, he was, like his father, a scourge of the Stuart cause. He is said to have gained the hand of Viscountess Primrose by boldly hiding in her house and his biography intriguingly reports him 'showing himself at her window'. Having gone into retirement to grow turnips and cabbages, he then accepted a field marshal's baton and commanded the British army until George II took over in person. He is said to have planted trees at his home at New Liston, west of Edinburgh, in groupings that represented regimental battle formations. A bit wrapped up in his work was Johnny.

A Splash of Tartan

Natural dyes used in old tartan gave the colours the special quality which left folk, from the Napoleonic battlefields to the temples of India, gasping. Here are the plants that were used to give particular colours:

Alder Tree Bark – *Black*
Dock Root – *Black*
Elderberry – *Blue*
Lichen – *Yellowish Brown*
Dulse – *Brown*
Blueberry – *Dark Brown*
Gall Nuts – *Dark Brown*
White Lichen – *Crimson*
Dark Lichen – *Dark Crimson*
Yellow Water Flag Root – *Grey*
Broom – *Green*
Whin – *Bark Green*
Sundew – *Purple*
Rue Root – *Red*
Bog Myrtle – *Yellow*
Bracken Root – *Yellow*
St John's Wort – *Yellow*

Size Matters

OK, here's a teaser – name Scotland's largest historical monu-ment. I suppose we'd all have a stab at Edinburgh Castle or Culloden Moor but we'd be way off the mark. The Antonine Wall, Britain's 'other' Roman wall, stretching from Old Kil-patrick on the River Clyde to Carriden on the Forth is 37 miles long and currently a candidate for World Heritage Site status.

The First-Ever Football Match Report

In 1815, the same year as the Battle of Waterloo, we encounter the first-ever piece of Scottish writing that could be said to resemble a football match report. Although not mentioned in the text, the author is thought to have been Sir Walter Scott, 'Wizard of the North', so-called, I believe, not because of his keepie-uppie skills but because of his literary talents.

There then follows a long list of distinguished spectators. You'll note that the idea that a team sheet might be of more interest than a roll call of the fans was still to come.

Ballantyne's Newspaper

4 December 1815

Dale of Yarrow 1 Selkirk 1

Half-time 0–1, estimated attendance 3000, estimated total team strengths 450, team marks of distinction – Selkirk, slips of fir and Yarrow, sprigs of heath; bad light stopped play.

On Monday, December 4, there was played, upon the extensive plain of Carterhaugh near the junction of the Ettrick and Yarrow, the greatest match at the ball which has taken place for many years. It was held by the people of the Dale of Yarrow against those of the parish of Selkirk; the former being brought to the field by the Right Hon. The Earl Home and the gallant Sutors by their chief magistrate, Ebenezer Clarkson Esq.

Both sides were joined by many volunteers from other parishes and the appearance of the various parties marching from their different glens to the place of rendezvous, with pipes playing and loud acclamations, carried back the coldest imagination to the old times when the Foresters assembled with the less peaceable purpose of invading the English territory or defending their own. The romantic character of the scenery aided the illusion, as well as the performance of a feudal ceremony previous to commencing the games.

The ball was thrown up between the parties by the Duke of Buccleuch and the first game was gained, after a severe conflict of an hour and a half duration, by the Selkirk men. The second game was still more severely contested, and after a close and stubborn contest of more than three hours with various fortune and much display of strength and agility on both sides, was was (sic) at length carried by the Yarrow men.

The ball should then have been thrown up a third time, but considerable difficulty occurred in arranging the voluntary auxiliaries from other parishes, so as to make the match equal and, as the day began to close, it was found impossible to bring the strife to an issue by playing a decisive game.

Both parties, therefore parted with equal honours but, before they left the ground, the Sheriff threw up his hat, and in Lord Dalkeith's name and his own challenged the Yarrow men, on the part of the Sutors to a match to be played upon the first convenient opportunity, with 100 picked men only on each side. The challenge was mutually accepted by Lord Home, on his own part and for Lord John Scott; and was received with acclamation by the players on both sides. The principal gentlemen took part with one side or the other, except the Duke of Buccleuch who remains neutral. Great play is expected and all bets are to be paid by the losers to the poor of the winning parish.

For the players themselves it was impossible to see a finer set of active and athletic young fellows than appeared on the field. But what we chiefly admired in their conduct was that, though several hundreds in number, exceedingly keen for their respective parties, and engaged in so rough and animated a contest, they maintained the most perfect good humour, and showed how unnecessary it is to discourage manly and athletic exercises among the common people, under pretext of maintaining subordination and good order.

We have only to regret that the great concourse of spectators rendered it difficult to mention the names of several players who distinguished themselves by feats of strength or agility. But we must not omit to record that the first ball was hailed [scored] by Robert Hall, mason in Selkirk, and the second by George Brodie, from Greatlaws, upon Aill-water.

Refreshments were distributed to the players by the Duke of Buccleuch's domestics, in a booth erected for the purpose; and no persons were allowed to sell ale or spirits on the field.

This report featured in *Ballantyne's Newspaper*. That these communal football matches in the first half of the nineteenth century were extraordinarily popular cannot be disputed. In 1836, a game between the Lord Provost and the 'Youth of Perth' and Lord Stormont and the 'Men of Scone' was abandoned due to the immense crowd of spectators who spilled on to the pitch.

Although Scott's effort must be regarded as the first genuine match report, we know football was being played at much earlier dates. A few years back, a cork-stuffed ball from the era of Mary, Queen of Scots was found in the rafters of Stirling Castle – and I know why it was left up there for four and a half centuries. The Courtiers XI were too scared to ask for their ball back in case they were dropped the following week – from the castle battlements.

Although the first official football clash between Scotland and England is dated in the nineteenth century, there is a tantalising reference to a game in 1599 at Bewcastle in Cumbria. A kind of disciplinary problem is suspected and a few red cards must have been shown because 'a number of Englishmen were taken prisoner and one man disembowelled' (but the good news is that, during touch-line treatment, he was sewn up again). Imagine the *Sportscene* highlights of that one!

Purposeful Pish [No. 1]

An important ingredient in the manufacture of gunpowder is saltpetre – found, among other places, in the residue of evaporated urine. Although Edinburgh had a deserved reputation for lobbing waste material oot the windae, many public-spirited citizens, in centuries past, would retain the contents of their overnight chanties for collection by the bucket-load on the morn.

When We Were All Onion Johnnies and Jeannies

LETTRES DE NARURALITÉ GÉNÉRALE POUR TOUTE LA
NATION D'ECOSSE PAR LE ROI LOUIS XII EN 1513
LOUIS PAR LA GRACE DE DIEU ROI DE FRANCE

Savoir faisons à tous presens et avenir, que, comme tous le temps et ancienneté, entre les rois de france et d'Ecosse & les princes et subjects es royeumes, y ait eu très estroite amitiè-confederation & allaince perpetuelle . . . et dernierement du temps du vivant de feu nostre très cher seigneur et cousin Charles vii, pleusieurs princes du dict royaume d'Ecosse, avec grand nombre de gens de la dicte nation, vinrent par deça pour aider a jetter et expulser hors du royaume les Anglois, qui detenoient & occupoient la plus part du royaume; lesouels exposerent leurs personnes si vertuesement contre les dicts Anglois, qu'ils furent chassés . . . et pour la grande loyalté & vertu qu'il trouva en eux, il en prit deux cents à la garde de sa personne . . . PARQUOI NOUS . . . ayant regard . . . à la grande loyalté et fidelité que toujours et sans avoir jamais varié a esté trouvé en eux AVONS RESOLU DECLARER ET ORDONNER tous ceaux du dict royaume d'Ecosse qui demeureront et decederont ci-après dans nos dicts royaumes . . . de quelque etat qu'ils soient . . . pourront acouerir en icelui tous biens, seigneuries et possessions qu'ils y pouront licitement acquerir comme s'ils etoient natifs de nostre dict royaume.

NATURALISATION OF FRENCHMEN
MARIE, QUEEN DOWAGER AND REGENE, 29th November 1558

"Because the maist Christian King of France has granted ane letter of naturalitié for him and his successors to all and sundrie Scotsmen – registered in the Chalmer of Compts – therefore the Queen's Grace, Dowager and Regent of this Realme and the Three estaites of the samin, thinks it guid and agreeable that the like letter of naturalitié be given and granted by the King and queen of Scotland . . . to all and sundrie the said maist Xtaine King of France subjects being or sall happen to be here in the Realme of Scotland in onie time to come with siklike privileges."

Some Simply Splendid Scottish Citizens . . .

Stirling's Stupendous Citizens

NAME	CLAIM TO FAME	DATE OF BIRTH
Billy Bremner	footballer	1942
Willie Carson	jockey	1942
Henry Drummond	theologian	1851
Duncan Ferguson	footballer	1971
Sir George Harvey	landscape painter	1806
Margaret Marshall	soprano	1949
Kirsty Young	newscaster	1969

Big Burghers in Brechin

NAME	CLAIM TO FAME	DATE OF BIRTH
Thomas Guthrie	theologian	1803
Peter Spence	chemist	1806
Sir Robert Watson-Watt	scientist	1892

Famous Forres Folk

NAME	CLAIM TO FAME	DATE OF BIRTH
Alexander Adam	teacher	1741
James Dick	philathropist	1743
Hugh Falconer	botanist	1808
Lord Strathcona	diplomat	1820

Renowned Rutherglen Residents

NAME	CLAIM TO FAME	DATE OF BIRTH
Sir Denis Brogan	historian	1900
Robbie Coltrane	actor	1950

Important Inverness Inhabitants

NAME	CLAIM TO FAME	DATE OF BIRTH
Jessie Kesson	novelist	1916
Elizabeth MacKintosh	author	1896
John McLennan	sociologist	1827
Sir James Swinburne	inventor	1858
Jane Waterston	missionary	1843

Distinguished Dunfermline Dudes

NAME	CLAIM TO FAME	DATE OF BIRTH
Stuart Adamson	rock star	1958
Ian Anderson	rock star / flautist	1947
Thomas Bower	psychologist	1941
Andrew Carnegie	philanthropist	1835
Sir Peter Chalmers	zoologist	1864
Charles I	king	1600
David II	king	1324
Barbara Dickson	singer	1947
Dorothy Dunnett	novelist	1923
James I	king	1394
Sir Kenneth Macmillan	choreographer	1929
Sir Joseph Paton	artist	1821
Moira Shearer	ballerina	1926

Noted Natives of Nairn

NAME	CLAIM TO FAME	DATE OF BIRTH
James Grant	explorer	1817
William Whitelaw	politician	1918

Historical Honchos of Haddington

NAME	CLAIM TO FAME	DATE OF BIRTH
Alexander II	king	1198
Walter Bower	chronicler	1385
Jane Carlyle	writer	1801
Sir William Gillies	artist	1898
John Knox	reformer	1513
Agnes Sampson	healer / witch	1592
Hew Scott	theologian	1791
Samuel Smiles	author	1812

Dignified Dwellers of Dumfries

NAME	CLAIM TO FAME	DATE OF BIRTH
Dougal Dixon	palaeontologist	1947
John Laurie	actor	1897
Dominic Matteo	footballer	1974
Sir John Richardson	explorer	1787
Kirsty Wark	journalist	1955

Significant Settlers from Shotts

NAME	CLAIM TO FAME	DATE OF BIRTH
Matthew Baillie	anatomist	1762
Margaret Herbison	politician	1907
Andrew Keir	actor	1926
John Millar	social historian	1735

Porky Pie, Pants on Fire — the Top Five Scottish Lies
(MOST OF THE BLAME RESTING WITH SIR WALTER 'C'MON-YOU-JACOBITES!' SCOTT)

1. Every genuine Scotsman wears a kilt and goes commando.
    Untruth: sadly we don't all have legs like Darius; thankfully
    we don't all have erses in the style of the Tartan Army which
    look as if they've been seeded by the Forestry Commission.

2. The centre of the universe is two-thirds of the way down a
box of Frosties, on the third shelf of the pantry of Mrs
Euphemia MacGrain, fifth floor flat, 1515 Dumbarton Road
Glasgow.
    Porky Pie: according to the laws of quantum mechanics it is
    has to be focused in the heart of every true Scot, in the
    homeland or in exile, a single point shared simultaneously
    and mystically by 50 million souls.

3. Only stout Highlanders were in the ranks of Bonnie Prince
Charlie's army at Culloden.
    Wrong on Both Counts: I know for a fact that it was a skinny
    wee guy from Shettleston, visiting his auntie at Dalcross, who
    actually held the Jacobite jaikets.

4. The noblest prospect a Scotchman ever sees is, as notorious
Scotophobe Dr Johnson suggested, the high road that takes
him to England.
    Only a Half-Truth: The high road to England takes you down
    the M74 from Glasgow to Gretna, right enough, but the
    noblest prospect is the return leg up the M74 from Gretna to
    Glasgow.

5. All Scots live in castles with the antlers of some poor deer set
above the door, a watercolour of the Young Chevalier on the
half-landing and a high tower from which they can shoot
pheasants if the fancy takes them.
    Fib: Most Scots do indeed make a castle of their home but they
    usually have a spy-hole in the door, a print of a bright orange
    Hawaiian sunset above the mantelpiece and in their tower you
    have to walk up fourteen floors because the lift is broken.

Gavin Hamilton's Strange Gift

Nowadays, the eighteenth-century painter Gavin Hamilton, from Lanark, is probably best known to that mysterious creature, the man or woman in the street, as the person who unearthed the biggest flowerpot in the world. This was The Warwick Vase from Hadrian's villa at Tivoli, the vase now being centrepiece of Glasgow's Burrell Gallery collection. Like so many Scottish artists and aristocrats in the 1700s, Hamilton went on the Grand Tour, a sort of combination of extended holiday and educational trip around the cities of Europe. It was in Rome that he chose to settle down.

In artistic terms, he was a neoclassicist, specialising in themes from Greek and Roman literature. To be truthful, and speaking as a novice in this field, I find most of his subjects on the 'heavy' side – the jolliest is probably the canvas of an episode from Roman history showing Agrippina returning with the ashes of her dead husband. Yeah, that cheery! His greatest works were scenes from Homer's *Iliad* and his fame spread far and wide.

Interestingly, it was a commission from Dr Johnson's Scots biographer James Boswell that saw Hamilton turn to Scottish history. This was to portray the abdication of Mary, Queen of Scots at Lochleven Castle. Frankly, it's another dark, brooding affair that does little to lift the spirits. One biographer suggested that he 'excelled in the grand and terrible'. Never was a truer word spoken.

Hamilton's knowledge of the antiquities of Rome eventually led him more or less to abandon painting in favour of more earthy, archaeological pursuits at which he was equally successful, making a series of important finds at sites around what had been the heart of the Roman Empire.

Two spooky wee stories illustrate the depth of his artistic talent. On a visit to Britain, he received a number of portrait commissions, one of these being to paint the Duchess of Hamilton. The portrait of the Duchess with the little greyhound jumping up and trying to attract her attention became well known from prints taken from it. But the story goes that there is another half-finished portrait of the Duchess by Hamilton. So stunning was the likeness, apparently, that the Duke took it from the easel and would never allow it to be completed in case the resemblance was lost.

Another of his commissions has an equally bizarre history. Maintaining the mournful theme, this painting represents Achilles dragging the body of Hector around the walls of Troy. The work, reckoned to be one of his masterpieces, was undertaken for the Duke of Bedford. After the painting was handed over, the Duke's son, the Marquis of Tavistock, was killed in a riding accident. He was thrown from his horse, caught his foot in the stirrup and was dragged to his death round the exterior of the house. The family were so struck by this strange precursor of the Marquis's death that they refused to look on Gavin's painting again and put it away in an attic before sending it to be sold at auction.

By the Way, some Weird Folklore

HATCHES

Scots parents expected children born in the early hours of the morning to be intellectually gifted – and just a bit on the wild side. On being removed from the birthing room, a newborn child must, by tradition, first be taken upstairs – even if this means climbing into the attic. Apparently, climbing on to a convenient chair would also do the trick. To prevent the newborn bairn being stolen by fairies, you have to walk sunwise seven times round your house. In a multi-storey, it means going up and down seven times in the lift or, if broken, seven times up and down the stairs. The name of the child must never be spoken until the baptism. Thereafter, believe me, you'll spend fifteen years or more shouting it at the top of your voice.

MATCHES

In Scotland weddings were most commonly held in winter but, if summer was the chosen season, then May was to avoided at all costs (echoes here, I suspect, of the Roman Festival of the Dead). Thursday, it seems, was an auspicious day to get married – closely followed by Tuesday as a second option. In the Northern Isles, according to the writer Ernest Marwick, it was important to marry with the 'moon growing and the tide flowing.'

Strange eve-of-wedding customs took place such as *fit-washin'* when a group of unmarried girls met at the bride's home to scrub her feet in a large wooden tub.

The bride and groom were often kidnap targets for the fairy folk around time of the wedding and the role of protecting the couple fell to the best man and maid of honour.

In Orkney, a watch would be kept on the 'wedding hoose' to ensure that no ill-disposed person walked round it 'against the sun'. If you did this carrying dried fish, it almost guaranteed that bride would have no milk for her first-born child.

The fiddler at wedding was traditionally offered the hot-tail pudding of a pig.

DISPATCHES

Don't get too hung up on the following supposed Scottish precursors of death. They are probably merely old wives' tales.

Simply be careful if you hear a bird tapping at the window or if you see a gull sitting on one leg on the chimney or if you hear an owl laughing. The bird is probably trying to etch a ditty on the window pane, the gull most likely had its other leg shot off by an air rifle and, as for the owl, if your face had been squashed flat, laughter is really all that's left to you – but you never know.

The wake is no longer part of the ceremonial of death in Scotland but, in centuries past, there were all sorts of rules relating to this practice. In the room where the body lay, all clocks had to be stopped and no fires lit. If a dog or cat passed (correct spelling?) over the body it had to be immediately slain.

Morag's Magical Scottish Kitchen
Fattie Cutties

3 cups of plain flour	4 oz currants
a pinch of bicarbonate of soda	a little milk
7 oz margarine	a pinch salt
3 tbsp granulated or castor sugar	

Melt the margarine and mix it with the milk. Mix all the dry ingredients together. Add the melted margarine and milk mixture to the dry ingredients and incorporate everything thoroughly.

Roll the mixture out quite thinly on a lightly greased board. Cut it into squares and cook them on a not too hot, lightly greased girdle for a couple of minutes on each side.

By the Way, Here's some Music Hall Magic

Theatre-going was a common pastime in the era before cinema, radio and TV and the fare on offer was nothing if not eclectic. Here are just a few of the delights featured in Scotland's palaces of pleasure.

Ted Marcelle – 'The Talkative Skater' (1880)
Rose Elliott – 'Singer of Sensible Songs' (1909)
Mlle Raffin and Her Performing Monkeys (1860)
Arthur Farren – The Greatest Female Impersonator (1854)
Sylvester's Working Head (1909)
La Milo – Exquisite Poseuse – A Daring Yet Chaste Show (1907)
The Battle of Bannockburn (1890)
Artistic Darkie Folk Songs (1920)
Miss Mabel de Vena, Club Swinger and Axe Manipulator (1840)
The Flying Potters (1930)
Mr Cartwright and His Musical Glasses (1810)
Blanche Cole with Her Hundred Pipers (1858)

The School of Hard Knox

You would never accuse the ordinary folk of Fife of being mean and cold-hearted, would you? However, it's maybe a different story when it comes to the gentry. In the nineteenth century, when the minister at West Anstruther (Anstruther Wester to the locals) asked the laird to assist with some finance to put a stove in the icy church because the congregating were chittering through the sermons, he was told, 'Warm them with your doctrine. John Knox never asked for a stove in his kirk.'

Scots Toasts

A Bottle and a Friend

Here's a bottle an' an honest friend,
Whit wid ye wish for mair, man?
Wha kens, before his life may end,
What his share may be o' care, man?

Then catch the moments as they fly,
And use them as ye ought, man,
Believe me, happiness is shy,
And comes no' ay when sought, man!

Robert Burns

- Whan we're gaun up the hill o' fortune, we ne'er meet a
  freend coming doon!

- To the Wee Man in the Velvet Jaiket!
  (*A Jacobite toast to the mole that dug the hole into which William
  of Orange's horse stuck its hoof and fell. King Billy suffered fatal
  injuries in this accident.*)

- May the moose ne'er leave your meal-pock wi' a tear in its
  ee!

- Up wi' yer glasses an' de'il tak' the hindmaist!

- To the cassin' o' the Wanchancie Covenant!
  (*Literally, 'To the casting off of the Unlucky Covenant', this was
  used by those who favoured the repeal of the 1707 Act of Union.*)

Just an Average Sort of Programme for the Fringe

A total of 12,940 performers were on the Fringe stages in 2003 and it is reckoned that it would take you four years and 143 days to see every Fringe performance back-to-back. Over the decades, some of the most outlandish shows on the planet have found their way to Edinburgh and, within the theatrical profession, it is widely agreed that, if you can succeed at the Fringe, you can succeed anywhere. On average, a third of the shows are world premieres. Here are a few of the stories that, over the years, have made the Fringe something very special:

Eight theatre groups turned up uninvited at the first Edinburgh International Festival in 1947 and the Fringe was born.

A theatrical orgy and love-in, due to be held in Princes Street in 1974 as part of the Fringe, was cancelled after rain set in and only one person turned up.

It's often asked if the Fringe is merely an artistic adventure. Not according to Scots actor Tom Conti who, in 1996, declared the essence of the Fringe to be 'cursing and swearing and everyone trying to get laid all the time. That's what it was and still is.'

In 1988, a woman demanded a refund after a performance of Sir Tom Stoppard's The Real Inspector Hound *because she had been seated behind a pillar. She was blind.*

In the 1960s, Edinburgh Councillor John Kidd, who had famously described all actors as 'big Jessies', appointed himself the arbiter of good taste for the city.

The English Shakespeare Company performed a selection of the bard's works on the top deck of a bus driving round the city. But only one enthusiastic fan saw the whole performance – he followed behind on a bicycle.

Leslie Bennie, Fringe Treasurer for twenty years, recalls a board outing with its intellectual chairman Dr Jonathan Miller to see the 'orchidaceous' conjuror Fay Presto. Miller confessed he fancied the girl in the fishnet tights, forcing Bennie to point out that the stunning 'she' was, in fact, a 'he'.

Self-styled comedian Peter Peanut had to be resuscitated in 1999 by a member of the audience after his trademark stunt of emptying a pack of peanuts up his nose backfired and one became lodged. The spectator, a medical student, carried out an improvised tracheotomy with a ballpoint pen.

Fringe Sunday, which encourages public involvement in the performing arts, has become an institution over the past three decades. At the first Fringe Sunday in 1981, organisers were stunned when 40,000 people crowded the streets. The event, which has moved to The Meadows now, attracts up to 200,000 people

Alistair Moffat, Fringe Administrator from 1976 to 1981, recalls that first day, 'There were no stages, just crowds of people around spaces where people were performing. I remember Ben Elton doing an incredible kind of rap thing on the steps of St Giles. Even if they only came up the town and walked down the High Street with their hands in their pockets they were taking part in the Fringe.'

Danger! — the Original Homebrew

The Scottish origins of homebrew reach back into prehistory. Archaeologists suggest that, around 2000 BC, residents of Rum, rather appropriately, concocted a fermented drink using the flowers of the heather plant and this heather ale (*leann fraoch*) is probably the oldest brew still commercially produced anywhere.

Who, exactly, gets the credit for introducing this idea is still a matter of contention but, by the time the Romans arrived on the scene, the use of native plants in fermented drinks was well established. It has been suggested that the beers made from darnel (corn weed) and bigg (barley) were often flavoured with hallucinogenic compounds of wormwood and ergot making the Picts fearsome and maybe a wee bit over-confident adversaries.

The recipe for heather brew was a secret closely guarded by the Picts according to a legend recounted by Robert Louis Stevenson. A Scots king trapped his Pictish counterpart and his son on the edge of a cliff and attempted to extort the secret recipe. The Pictish king agreed to spill the beans if his son was spared torture and killed with mercy. The Scots king agreed to this and over the edge went the boy. However, the devious Pict turned to the Scot proclaiming, 'Fire shall never avail, here dies in my bosom the secret of heather ale!' So saying, he threw himself over the precipice dragging the Scot with him.

Fortunately someone, somewhere had had enough wisdom to etch the formula on to a Class II symbol stone, which lies in the potting shed of the descendants of the Pictish kings, somewhere in the Mearns. For the adventurous amongst you here is the recipe:

HEATHER ALE

1 gallon canister (an old Pictish measure!) of heather tips

2 gallons of water (from an east flowing stream)

$^{1}/_{2}$ oz hops

1 lb of golden syrup (What do you mean you've never heard of the Pictish sugar industry?)

1 oz ginger

1 oz yeast

Gather the heather tips when in full bloom. Put them in a large pan and cover with water. Bring to the boil and simmer for one hour. Strain the liquid through a muslin cloth into a large bowl and set it aside.

Mix together the water, hops, golden syrup and ginger and boil for 20 minutes. Strain into the heather water. Once cooled to lukewarm, add the yeast and leave to rest for 24 hours.

Your ale is now ready to bottle. Carefully collect the clear liquid only – leave the yeasty sediment at the bottom. Pour it into sterilised bottles and cork. Leave the ale for 2–3 days before drinking – if you can restrain yourself for that long!

Feel free to experiment. Add anything you fancy just before the fermentation stage. Prior to a government intervention in the 1400s brewers did exactly this, using everything from onions to chickens, often with deleterious results. More pleasing was the introduction of pine and spruce ales by the Vikings. These products were said to increase your sex drive and improve your chances of conceiving twins. Pine ales were carried by the explorer James Cook on his voyages to prevent scurvy.

Nettles, seaweed, gooseberries, elderberries and even the sap of silver birch trees have been used to flavour alcoholic products – so get out into the back garden and check out your homebrew resources.

A Load of Old Bull?

Bored by nights in front of the telly or down at the pub? Then why not take up *taghairm*? This ancient Highland practice involves wrapping yourself in an ox hide and spending the night behind a waterfall in an attempt to achieve devine inspiration.

Apparently *taghairm* can also be applied to a rather more sinister custom which involved spit-roasting a live cat. As poor Fluffy miaowed her way to that great cat basket in the sky, those in the know would interpret her cries as instructions from the gods.

The Scots Family and its Complexities

And so ye see auld Pittodles, when his third wife deed, he got mairrit upon the Laird o' Blaithershins' aughteenth daughter, that was sister to Jemima, that was mairrit till Tam Flumexer, that was first and second cousin to the Pittodleses, whase brother became laird efterward, an' mairrit Blaithershins Baubie – an' that way Jemima becam' in a kind o' way her ain neice an' her ain aunty an' we used to say her good bruther was mairrit to his ain grannie.

Hislop's *Book of Scottish Anecdote*

The Death and Life of the Scottish Lobster

Lobsters today are one of the great delicacies from Scottish waters, having risen from being the staple fare of the humble shore-dweller to become the target of the top restaurants in major European cities. If you've always fancied preparing and sampling this black-enamelled bastion of the deep but felt intimidated by the procedure then you're moment has come:

When buying a lobster to eat at home, look for a lively and fresh specimen. To test this at the fishmonger's, pick up the lobster by the sides (ensuring that the pincers are taped!). When you do this, the lobster's response should be to tuck its tail tightly underneath its body. After selecting your lobster, get it covered and in the fridge as soon as you get home. Covering the lobster with a damp cloth or newspaper will keep it alive but it must be cooked within 12–18 hours. Lobsters will die swiftly from osmotic stress if they are kept in fresh water, so keep them out of the bath.

The next section is not for the squeamish. Should the lobster go into the pot dead (recently) or alive? Plunging the live lobster straight into the pot will certainly cause a power of thrashing and, in some cases (personal experience here), the lobster is liable to jump out of the pot and run across the kitchen, to the hopping chorus of three screaming children.

At any rate, chefs would not recommend live-boiling as the muscles tense on hitting the water, resulting in chewy meat. Tail movement is part of the escape-reflex response found in lobsters and crayfish and may be observed for up to a minute and a half after immersion. Another disturbing side effect of boiling alive is that the lobster appears to 'scream' after you drop it in the pot. This is not really a cry for help but trapped air escaping from small fissures in the shell.

As you might expect, there are welfare issues associated with this method of killing. Research indicates that the lobster has a very simple nervous system, similar to that of an insect, suggesting that lobsters are unlikely to feel pain. Despite this, most cooks prefer to kill the lob before cooking.

This can achieved by placing the lobster in the freezer an hour before cooking or, even quicker, plunging a sharp knife down behind the lobster's eyes. Other methods of killing, tested by the University of Maine, include hypnosis, pot steaming, freezing, drowning, spiking, splitting and tailing. Now these students must be a fun bunch!

Once the dirty deed is done and the lobster is in the pot, one way or another, bring the water back to the boil, then turn it down to a simmer. Cover and cook for five minutes for the first pound and then one more minute for each additional pound. After this time, take out the lobster and allow it to drain. Twist off the claws and crack each claw with a nutcracker. Separate the tailpiece from the body. Bend and break the flippers from the tailpiece and push out the meat with a fork. Get into the body of the lobster to take out the remaining meat.

Lobster Lore and Learning

Lobsters are crustaceans with five pairs of legs and a curling tail

The North Atlantic lobster carries the Latin name *Homarus Vulgaris*

Naturally blue in colour, they turn red when boiled (Wouldn't we all?)

Lobster shells have been found in kitchen middens 10,000 years old

Despite their beady eyes they have very poor vision

Even in the 1700s, Orkney lobsters found their way on to London dining tables

They carry their skeleton outside their body and have been around for 200 million years

They grow by moulting, shedding their exoskeletons, increasing in weight by up to 25% with each moult

In the first five years of life, a lobster may moult up to 25 times

Lobsters seen in Scottish fishmongers generally weigh between one and two pounds

The world's largest lobster, caught in 1977 in Nova Scotia, was 44 lbs and four feet long!

There is a legal minimum size for lobsters, measured by a special gauge

Lobsters have their teeth in their stomach, their kidneys in their heads and their noses in their feet

They are quite literally made inside out and upside down

They will happily be cannibals – hence the need for taped claws when two or more are kept together in storage tanks

Lobsters are naturally left- or right-handed, with one larger claw and a smaller, sweeter claw

They have the uncanny ability to cast off limbs and regrow them

Lobster meat has a high proportion of glycogen, a polysaccharide that converts into glucose, and it's this that gives their sweet and succulent flesh

Scotland's Scariest Roundabouts

Scary Location	Scary Points Out of Ten	Scary Comment
Haudagain Roundabout, Great Northern Road, Aberdeen	10/10	Truly terrifying – don't go there
Kingsway / Forfar Road Roundabout, Dundee	8/10	Keep your wits about you
Gogar Roundabout, Edinburgh City Bypass	7/10	None but the brave
Sheriffhall Roundabout Edinburgh City Bypass	7/10	A true test of nerves
Whirlies Roundabout, East Kilbride	7/10	Full-size real life dodgems
Auchenkilns Roundabout, A80, at Cumbernauld	7/10	Busy, busy, busy – far TOO busy
Raith Interchange, M74, near Hamilton	7/10	A roundabout way too far

How to Survive Scottish Roundabouts

1. Look out for pedestrians and cyclists. Roundabouts are generally safer than the open road for drivers because speed is lower but, for bikers and walkers, they are zones of peril.
2. One of the greatest failings of Scottish drivers on roundabouts is the lack of indication, especially when leaving the roundabout, and this is the cause of countless

bumps – so let people know where you're going in good time.

3. Stay in the same lane and don't wander about across the carriageway – but be aware that local custom might differ from standard driving practice on some roundabouts.

4. Because traffic is so tightly packed on approaches and on the roundabouts themselves, always expect the unexpected.

5. Never find yourself trying to squeeze your way round beside a bus or an articulated vehicle – most longer vehicles need a wide arc to negotiate tight urban roundabouts so always give them plenty of room.

6. Watch the approach signs carefully so that you can take up the appropriate position in plenty of time.

Haggii-ography – a Beginner's Guide

It's become something of tradition these days for visitors to Scotland, particularly our American cousins, to demand confidential information about the exotic lifestyle of the haggis. And it's kind of expected that you produce the goods. As a handy guide to keeping the tourists content, you can perm any five from these twelve haggis 'facts' and you'll send them away happy:

The haggis is one of Scotland's best-loved native species/dishes

A shy creature of the heather-clad hills, the haggis roams in herds, foraging for heather, berries, neeps and tatties

The technical collective noun for a group of haggii (never, never haggises!) is a 'humph' but they are most often referred to as a herd

Haggii live in burrows, hibernating for most of the year to avoid midges, twitchers, Munro-baggers and to dodge the haggis hunters but venturing out on Hogmanay and January 25 for mating

Because all haggii are either right- or left-legged, depending on the lie of their natal hillside, they have evolved an 'uphill' leg shorter than the 'downhill' leg, allowing a natural stability while foraging

Hunting method: hunters surround the haggii humph, causing the beasties to huddle together. They then drive them across the hillside before forcing a sudden change of direction. The effect of the change of direction is to cause the humph to tumble spectacularly, presenting an easy target for the hunter

Haggii are the main component in the celebration of the bard, Robert Burns, on January 25 each year

It is traditional for the haggii to be piped in although a rousing chorus of the haggis anthem 'Five Hundred Miles' will suffice

Before serving, Burns's poem 'Address to a Haggis (on seeing one on a lady's bonnet at church)' is recited

For maximum dramatic effect, the person cutting into the haggis does so at the 'An' cut you up wi' ready slight' line in the third verse!

It's worth also mentioning that, such is the rarity of the haggis, you are unlikely ever to see one roaming free. However, as a consolation, you might offer this foolproof 'Build Your Own Haggis' recipe which can easily be created at home and makes a useful substitute if you're staging your own Burns supper. Be warned though – this is not for the faint of heart:

TRADITIONAL HAGGIS

1 sheep's stomach, empty
cold salted water
1 sheep's pluck – the heart, liver and lights (lungs)
1 lb lightly toasted pinhead oatmeal
8 oz finely chopped suet
4 large onions, finely chopped
1–2 tablespoons of salt
pepper
1 tablespoon of ground allspice
1 tablespoon of mixed herbs
lemon juice
vinegar
pinch of cayenne pepper

Wash the stomach in cold water and then soak it in cold salted water for 8–10 hours. Place the pluck in a large pot and cover with cold water. The windpipe should be hung over the side of the pot with a container below to collect any drips. Simmer the pluck for two hours and leave it to cool. Retain the liquid.

Mince the pluck meat and mix it with the toasted oatmeal. Add half a pint of the liquid in which the pluck was boiled, suet, onions and season. Mix well, add the allspice, herbs, lemon juice, vinegar and cayenne and mix again so that everything is well incorporated. Fill the stomach with the mixture, leaving room for expansion.

Press out the air (important) and sew up the haggis. (Knowing a doctor or seamstress whose services you can call on at this stage is handy.) Prick the haggis a few times with a needle, place it in a pan of boiling water and simmer for three hours.

Now, if that doesn't put a halt to the questions, nothing will!

By the Way, Lost Your Clan?

It does happen, you know. Out-and-out Scots, with ever so slightly bizarre names like Hewitson, suddenly find themselves missing a clan, lacking a Highland connection, wanting, desperately, to be part of the great tartan extravaganza. Here's a wee helping hand for some of the more obscurely named amongst us.

Obscure Name	Connected Clan
Clanachan	Maclean
Federith	Sutherland
Greusach	Farquharson
Griesck	Macfarlane
Hewitson	Macdonald
Lair	Maclaren
Maccaa	Macfarlane
MacGilvernock	Graham
MacInstalker	Macfarlane
MacO'Shannaig	Macdonald
MacWhannell	Macdonald
Meyners	Menzies
O'Drain	Macdonald
O'Shaig	Macdonald
Raith	Macrae
Rome	Johnstone
Sorely	Cameron, Macdonald
Tawesson	Campbell
Train	Ross

Seems like the Macdonalds are the most accommodating towards the dispossessed – they're even prepared to offer sanctuary to the Hewitsons!

On Top of the Heap

Genealogy. For most of the past twenty years, I feel as if I've been stumbling through a forest of family trees and local histories in search of quirky stories of the Scots overseas. One stunning fact that has left me with an inferiority complex is that, almost without exception, everyone I've encountered has managed, somehow, to track down an illustrious ancestor. In my correspondence, you'll find folk who happily claim descent from Malcolm Canmore, by way of Mary, Queen of Scots and Rob Roy Macgregor. It rather reminds me of the way in which everyone who goes to a séance ends up talking to Marie Antoinette or Sitting Bull – eerie. Alongside this, my own family history appears unspectacular. Sheep-stealing has been mentioned and that's about as exciting as it gets.

You'll find throwaway lines in many of the family biographies on my shelves. I quote from just one: 'Alexander Macgruder, an officer in the army of Charles II, who was captured at the Battle of Worcester in 1651, was sent to Virginia as a prisoner-of-war . . . he was descended from Alpin, King of Scotland, 834.' Yes, it's as easy as that.

Now, I understand why the folk in the Scots diaspora are desperate to get their origins established – there just isn't enough history out there in the 'colonies'. However, I've always been a bit cynical about this illustrious ancestor business – that was until I got down to the mathematics of it. Statistics cannot lie. The startling truth is that we all probably did have an illustrious – or notorious – antecedent.

Let's unpick this. Working on the basis of each generation being roughly twenty-five years and assuming no inter-family marriage (OK, so cousin Mary *can* look awfully attractive after an evening on the heather ale), if you go back a century, you will already have a total of thirty ancestors (two parents, four grandparents, eight great-grandparents and 16 great-great-grandparents). Soon the figures begin to pile up spectacularly. Tracking back, a child born in the year 2000 will have half-a-million ancestors by the time we get back to the Scottish Reformation in the mid 1500s.

Chances are, indeed, that, among that lot, you're going to have a few celebrities – maybe even the odd king – but also, to be honest, a fair share of murderers, villains, out-and-out bastards (with whatever meaning of the word you care to apply) and, I would, guess the odd sheep-stealer.

The following table is a mind-blower. I thought I'd stop at a billion ancestors simply because, beyond that, the research might get unmanageable!

Generation	Year Born	Relationship to You	Ancestor Total
1	2000	You	2
2	1975	Parents	4
3	1950	Grandparents	8
4	1925	Great-Grandparents	16
5	1900	Great- x 2 Grandparents	32
6	1875	Great- x 3 Grandparents	64
7	1850	Great- x 4 Grandparents	128
8	1825	Great- x 5 Grandparents	256
9	1800	Great- x 6 Grandparents	512
10	1775	Great- x 7 Grandparents	1,024
11	1750	Great- x 8 Grandparents	2,048
12	1725	Great- x 9 Grandparents	4,096
13	1700	Great- x 10 Grandparents	8,192
14	1675	Great- x 11 Grandparents	16,384
15	1650	Great- x 12 Grandparents	32,768
16	1625	Great- x 13 Grandparents	65,536
17	1600	Great- x 14 Grandparents	131,072
18	1575	Great- x 15 Grandparents	262,144
19	1550	Great- x 16 Grandparents	524,288
20	1525	Great- x 17 Grandparents	1,048,576
21	1500	Great- x 18 Grandparents	2,097,152
22	1475	Great- x 19 Grandparents	4,194,304
23	1450	Great- x 20 Grandparents	8,388,608
24	1425	Great- x 21 Grandparents	16,777,216
25	1400	Great- x 22 Grandparents	33,554,432
26	1375	Great- x 23 Grandparents	67,108,864
27	1350	Great- x 24 Grandparents	134,177,728
28	1300	Great- x 25 Grandparents	268,435,456
29	1275	Great- x 26 Grandparents	536,870,912
30	1250	Great- x 27 Grandparents	1,073,741,824

Scotland's Most Notorious Letter?

On February 13, 1692 the massacre of the MacIan MacDonalds of Glencoe was authorised by William of Orange after the clan chief – delayed by snowstorms – had failed to meet a deadline for swearing allegiance to the new Protestant king. In the slaughter, thirty-eight clansfolk were killed by a force led by Campbell of Glenlyon who had been lodging with the MacDonalds. For Glenlyon, this was a no-win situation as the letter clearly states. His choice was mass murderer or traitor:

To Captain Robert Campbell of Glen Lyon
'for their majesties service'

Sir,

You are hereby ordered to fall upon the rebels, the M'Donalds of Glencoe, and putt all to the sword under seventy. You are to have special care that the old fox and his sons doe upon no account escape your hands. You are to secure all avenues that no man may escape. This you are to put in execution att five o'clock in the morning precisely and by that time, or very shortly after it, I'll strive to be att you with a stronger party. If I doe not come to you att five, you are not to tarry for me but to fall on. This is by the king's special command for the good and safety of the country that these miscreants be cut off root and branch. See that this be putt in execution without feud or favour else you may expect to be treated as not true to the king's government, nor a man fitt to carry a commission in the king's service. Expecting you not fail in the fulfilling hereof as you love yourself. I subscribe these with my hand,

Robert Duncanson,
Ballacholis,
February 12, 1692

Do the Fairies — and Yourself — a Big Favour

Now, I have to admit that fairy rings, those strange circular grassy shapes you encounter in lonely meadows in the half-light of dusk, have not played a major part in my life. Until now, I haven't danced around them, swept them or, to be honest, given them much consideration. As they say, the world is too much with us of late for that sort of a cairry-oan. However, having uncovered this salutary little ditty from another time, when we were closer to the old magic, I am perhaps having second thoughts.

> *He wha tills the fairies' green*
> *Nae luck again shall hae.*
> *An' he wha spills the fairies' ring*
> *Betide him want an' wae.*
>
> *But wha gaes by the fairy ring*
> *Nae dule nor pine shall see,*
> *An' he who cleans the fairy ring,*
> *An easy death shall see.*

If you see me out on the green wi' the brush, you'll know what I'm up to.

The Most Bizarre Auld Scots Exclamation

A' ee oo

(It's a' wan tae me)

When Orkney Was at the Centre of the North Atlantic World

In the Early Middle Ages when trade and travel followed the great sea highways, the Earldom of Orkney, still very much part of the Norse rather than the Scottish world, stood at the hub of this ocean empire.

Ca' Canny wi' the Satire, Robbie!

Three lawyers' tongues, turned inside out,
Wi' lies seamed like a beggar's clout;
Three priests' hearts, rotten, black as muck,
Lay stinking, vile, in every neuk.

Robert Burns

These are four lines excised from the original version of 'Tam o' Shanter' and they are seldom, if ever, seen nowadays. Robert Burns is such a national hero, a legendary Scottish icon, that it's occasionally nice to hear that he was fallible and happy to be guided, just like the rest of us.

In the year 1793, 'Tam o' Shanter', arguably his most famous and well-loved poem, underwent a strange, if minor, makeover which involved something uncomfortably like an accommodation of political correctness.

In 1791, Alexander Fraser Tytler, an Edinburgh advocate, Professor of Universal History at Edinburgh University and a man of letters, got hold of a sheet of Grose's *Antiquities* in which was printed the very first public version of 'Tam o' Shanter'. He was already familiar with Burns and wrote a letter to the poet praising the work in glowing terms, particularly the bard's description of the witches' Sabbath in Kirk Alloway in which he said Burns displayed 'a power of imagination that Shakespeare himself could not have exceeded.' His blood, he declared, had run cold on reading these stanzas and he predicted that Burns would go on to eclipse the greatest poets of his day.

Ah, but, the learned professor did have one little reservation. In the scenes when Burns is describing the paraphernalia of the Sabbath, the bard turns his wit briefly on the legal profession and the clergy. Said Tytler:

the descriptive part might perhaps have been better closed than the four lines which succeed, which, though good in themselves, yet, as they derive all their merit from the satire they contain are here rather misplaced among the circumstances of pure horror.

Burns responded by letter and resolved that 'the hit at the lawyer and the priest, I shall cut out'. When the 1793 edition of the poem appeared, the offending lines were missing.

In a first draft, that was also cut, Burns had criticised doctors too. Thomas Crawford, an expert on the work of Burns, says that this group of professional people were stock figures who were regularly the butt of eighteenth-century social criticism.

French Words what we Have Pinched!

FRENCH	AULD SCOTS	NEW SCOTS
Assiette	Ashet	Plate
Armoire	Aumrie	Cupboard
Bon aller	Bonally	Farewell
Boisson	Boss	Drink
Calendre	Calander	Mangle
Fouace	Fadge	Tattie scone
Facher	Fash	Annoy
Gardez l'eau	Gardyloo	Here comes the pish
Gigot	Gigot	Leg of lamb
Groseille	Grosset	Gooseberry
Jalouser	Jalouse	Suspect
Commere	Kimmer	Gossip
Raifort	Refforts	Horseradish
Recueil	Ruckle	Collection
Asperger	Spairge	Sprinkle
Etuve	Stovies	Stewed tatties
Cibo	Sybo	Spring onion
Tasse	Tassie	Cup

Heading Home . . .

By yon bonnie banks and by yon bonnie braes,
Where the sun shines bright on Loch Lomond,
Where me and my true love were ever wont tae gae,
On the bonnie, bonnie banks of Loch Lomond.

REFRAIN
O, you tak' the high road and I'll tak' the low road,
And I'll be in Scotland afore ye,
But me and my true love will never meet again,
On the bonnie, bonnie banks of Loch Lomond.

This song, although loved by overseas Scots, is generally regarded, by home-based Caledonians, as an example of gushy sentimentality. In fact, it's a wonderful and moving tale that weaves Celtic folklore with Jacobite history and certainly deserves a better public reception.

Celtic legend suggested that, when someone meets with death in a foreign land, their spirit makes its way back to the place of its birth by the underground fairy way – the 'low road'. In 1745, several wounded Jacobites had to be left at Carlisle as the army headed north to its final defeat at Culloden. The song, 'The Bonnie, Bonnie Banks o' Loch Lomond', is said to have been written at the period and tells of the fates of two Scottish Jacobite prisoners. One of them was released and took the 'high road' home to Scotland whilst the other was executed took the 'low road'. The release of one and the execution of the other were timed for the same hour and the dead man, travelling the 'low road', would speed home along the spiritual M74, arriving home long before his companion who would have to tramp mile after weary mile to cross the Border.

Ah Was Taking my Dog out the Other Day When . . .

It would have been around the middle of last century when I first encountered Charles Thomas McKinnon Murray and his jokes. Chic Murray's style of humour has been variously described as droll, absurd, surreal, lugubrious and woebegone. One thing is for sure – his style was as Clydeside as a shipyard riveter's sweaty socks. There were no half measures with Chic's humour – you either loved it or hated it. With his obligatory bunnet and hangdog expression, he was a unique phenomenon. Chic was the master of melancholy and king of the crest-fallen.

Almost without thinking, as if overtaken by some sort of demonic, comic possession and to the dismay of my children, I find myself regularly indulging in some of Chic's master-strokes. Gems like 'You know what they say about stamp collecting? Philately will get you nowhere!' or the ubiquitous and punishing 'Is that a doughnut or a meringue?' tumble unbidden from my mouth.

Most people will remember Chic for his role as the head-master in the 1981 movie, *Gregory's Girl*. However, to let younger folk sample some of his skills and to remind the more mature audience of what they've been missing since Chic passed on to the great music hall in the sky in 1985, here's my personal top ten Chic Murray jokes, faithfully noted over the years.

So there I was lying in the gutter. A man stopped and asked, 'What's the matter? Did you fall over?'
So I said, 'No, I've a toffee bar in my pocket and I was just trying to break it.'

My parents were wonderful – always there with a ready compromise. My sister wanted a cat for a pet and I wanted a dog so they bought a cat and taught it to bark.

I was taking my dog out the other day when I met this chap who asked where I was going. The dog was foaming at the mouth so I explained I was on the way to the vet to have him put down. He asked if it was mad to which I replied that it wasn't exactly pleased about it.

This chap said to me, 'If you look over there you'll see Dumbarton Rock.'
Well, I looked for twenty minutes and the thing never moved an inch.

I first met my wife in the tunnel of love. She was digging it at the time.

My girlfriend's a redhead – no hair, just a red head.

I went to the butcher's to buy a leg of lamb. 'Is it Scotch?' I asked.
Said the butcher in reply, 'Are you going to talk to it or eat it?'
Says I, 'In that case, have you got any wild duck?'
'No,' he responded, 'but I've one I could aggravate for you.'

I met this cowboy with a brown paper hat, paper waistcoat and paper trousers. He was wanted for rustling.

If something's neither here nor there, then where the hell is it?

It's a small world – but I wouldn't want to have to paint it.

My father was a simple man. My mother was a simple woman. You see the result standing in front of you — a simpleton.

Turning Yourself Into a Hare

The name Isobel Gowdie, from Auldearn in Nairn, is almost forgotten in Scotland today. But, in 1662, she created a sensation with her detailed confession to charges of witchcraft when she appeared before a tribunal composed of the sheriff of the county, the parish minister and nine local gentlemen. The full confessions of Isobel and her fellow coven member, Janet Braidhead, are considered by many to be the most remarkable witch cases on record. There is no note of the outcome of the case but the general consensus seems to be that the pair were burned at the stake.

Apart from the familiar stories of relationships with Auld Nick, dancing in the kirkyard and casting spells, the really scary part of the tribunal report describes how the women shunned the need for the witches' traditional mode of transport – the broomstick – claiming they had the ability to transform themselves into hares, cats and crows.

Isobel told of an adventure while she was in the guise of hare. She then stunned the tribunal by reciting the spell that brought about her transformation and restoration. It ran:

> *I sall go intill a hare,*
> *Wi' sorrow, sich and mickle care;*
> *And I sall do in the devil's name,*
> *Aye, till I be fetched hame.*

Isobel revealed how, on one occasion, about daybreak, she was heading for Auldearn, in the guise of a hare, when she encountered Patrick Papley's servants, heading for their work and complete with their pack of hounds. Hounds being hounds, they got on to Isobel's case forthwith and chased her across the fields.

She declared, 'I ran very long but was forced, being weary,

at last, to take my own house. The door being left open, I ran in behind a chest and the hounds followed in; but they went to the other side of the chest and I was forced to run forth again and wan into ane other house and there took leisure to say:

> Hare, hare, God send thee care!
> I am in a hare's likeness now,
> But I sall be a woman even now!
> Hare, hare, God send thee care!

And so she was transformed to human form again. Isobel explained that, although, from time to time, the dogs did sink their teeth into the witches, 'when we turn to our shape we will have bits and rives and scarts in our bodies but we will not be killed'.

Now the chances of you being chased round Auldearn these days by Patrick Papley's hounds are remote but, if this spell does the business for you and you get yourself into hare mode, then my advice would be to stay well clear of the speeding traffic on the A96. That could turn out to be a very bad hare day!

By the Way, a Very Different Song of the Clyde

There are now said to be over 50,000 people employed in various aspects of the tourist industry in the Glasgow area. Incredibly that is more than the number of people working in Clydeside's shipyards at their industrial peak.

Scotland's International Twins

Scotland has been a nation of wanderers for centuries and town twinning has been a feature of our municipal life for most of the second half of the twentieth century and into the twenty-first. As a result, lasting relationships have been built between Scottish towns and local authorities and their counterparts throughout the world. Cultural, educational and civic exchanges have brought people closer, letting nation blether unto nation.

There are obviously more outlandish and less official links such as the proposed tie-up between Largo in Fife and Robinson Crusoe Island in the Pacific islands group of Juan Fernandez. Four hundred miles off the South American coast, this was where Fifer Alexander Selkirk is thought to have been marooned for four years in the early 1700s, providing Daniel Defoe with the inspiration for his famous castaway story.

Many of the larger towns and cities have impressive batches of 'twins' but here are some of our Scottish communities and their more unusual international pals – a sort of A–Z of 'hands across the sea':

ALBUFEIRA (PORTUGAL)	DUNFERMLINE
AYR	ST GERMAIN-EN-LAYE (FRANCE)
BRECHIN	CASTELNAU- LE-LEZ (FRANCE)
BULAWAYO (ZIMBABWE)	ABERDEEN
CARLETON PLACE (CANADA)	COMRIE
CULROSS	VEERE (NETHERLANDS)
DALIAN (CHINA)	GLASGOW
DALKEITH	DALKEITH (AUSTRALIA)
ELGIN	LANDSHUT (GERMANY)
FLEKKEFJORD (NORWAY)	BURNTISLAND
FRASERBURGH	BRESSUIRE (FRANCE)
GOREY (IRELAND)	OBAN

Grangemouth	La Porte (USA)
Hawick	Bailleul (France)
Hordaland (Norway)	Orkney
Inchture	Fleac (France)
Isle Sur La Sorgue (France)	Penicuik
Jedburgh	Malestroit (France)
Jouy-en-Josas (France)	Bothwell
Kilmarnock	Santa Coloma de Gramenet (Spain)
Kyoto (Japan)	Edinburgh
Lochaber	Sydney Milnes (Canada)
Lubin (Poland)	Falkirk
Monasterboice (Ireland)	Monifeith
Musselburgh	Rosignano Maritimo (Italy)
Nablus (Palestine)	Dundee
North Berwick	Kerteminde (Denmark)
Oban	Laurinburg (USA)
Orchies (France)	Kelso
Peterhead	Aalesund (Norway)
Pskov (Russia)	Perth
Redlands (USA)	Inverness
Ross & Cromarty	Krosno (Poland)
Schweinfurt (Germany)	Motherwell
Shetland	Vagsoy (Norway)
Thurso	Heusden Zolder (Belgium)
Trelleborg (Sweden)	Buckhaven & Methil
Volvic (France)	Kirriemuir
Watermaal Bosvoorde (Belgium)	Annan
Wick	Klaksvik (Faroe Islands)
Xian (China)	Edinburgh
Yvetot (France)	Clydesdale
Zagan (Poland)	Duns

We're Still Waiting, Tam!

Thomas the Rhymer was a thirteenth-century wordsmith whose reputation as a prophet was regularly referred to throughout the later Middle Ages. He claimed to have spent the obligatory seven years in Elfland required for seers. Of all his prophecies there is one that I find particularly tantalising. It runs:

> *York was, London is but Edinburgh shall be*
> *The greatest o' the three.*

By Butter Yellow Candlelight

The American film industry was transformed in the 1920s by Andrew Kennedy, an Orcadian who invented and developed a system of portable lighting which led to the start of location filming. His invention, which he named 'Orcadia', could deliver two and a half million units of candlepower.

No such technological advance was necessary for seventh-century St Fillan who is associated with Fife and Perthshire and who unquestionably saved his abbey a fortune in candles if the legends are to be believed. During long nights transcribing the scriptures, a miraculous light radiated from his left hand, illuminating the corrie-fisted one's immediate working area. Neat, eh? His amazing hand became a revered relic and was with the victorious Scots at Bannockburn. A similar story is told of Columba of Iona.

Throwing Together a Sheiling

The caber-tossing event is one of the most popular at Highland Games across the globe in the twenty-first century and is said, by some sources, to originate from the practice of house construction where young men competed to toss roof timbers into place on the roofs of the sheilings. Every caber was required to come to rest as near to the straight position giving the basis of present day rules.

Geordie is the classic tale of a wee Scottish boy who takes up body-building (and, of course, eats up his porridge oats), becomes a Highland Games hero and wins an Olympic gold medal. The story was actually written in Canada by Dundee-born David Waler after he went to live in New Brunswick in 1948.

Some Highland Games events in the late 1700s and early 1800s were of very dubious antiquity and authenticity. Macdonell of Glengarry (1773–1828), the so-called 'Last of the Chiefs' (although Queen Victoria might have something to say about that) devised a contest in which servants tried to rip the legs from deceased cattle with their bare hands. On one occasion, this bizarre spectacle is said to have lasted five hours.

By the Way, You Can Keep Your Damned Watery Music, Geordie

Georg Friedric Händel, a devout Hanoverian, as you would expect, wrote the anthem *See the Conquering Hero Come* in tribute to the heroic deeds performed by Butcher Cumberland during and after the Battle of Culloden.

Making Yourself Invisible

The cloak of invisibility has always been a bit of a Holy Grail for alchemists and wizards down through the ages. Scotland, however, has what we are told is a foolproof method for losing your corporeal self.

Before disclosing this ancient formula and incurring the wrath of everyone from the Royal Society for the Protection of Birds to the medical profession, I should tell you that I personally have a foolproof ability to disappear. In any trendy, busy, noisy bar, I can stand for half-an-hour, quite invisible to the bar staff, as I wait to order until one of my tall pals or gallus gals steps in. But to business . . .

TO MAKE YOURSELF INVISIBLE

1. Take two eggs from a raven's nest and boil them
2. Return them to the nest
3. The birds, finding the eggs have been tampered with, will fly away
4. They will return each with a piece of crystal in their beaks
5. Climb to the nest and secure a crystal
6. Sook it and you'll see but be not seen!
7. Return it to your pocket and you will once more be visible

If this fails, then, as an alternative, catch fern seeds as they fall at midnight on St John's Eve, June 24. Eerily this was also the eve of the Battle of Bannockburn in 1314. Has the 'invisibility factor' in the Scottish victory been given proper consideration? Why were the Scottish army seen on hands and knees in the hills around Stirling on the eve of battle? Were they praying? Or perhaps gathering some very special seeds?

Hume Didn't Know His Ossian from His Elbow

James MacPherson, a Ruthven schoolmaster, enjoyed spectacular success with his *Tales of Ossian*, a collection of 'genuine' Gaelic folk tales that had taken Romantic old Europe by storm – even if they failed to impress London critics like that auld sourpuss Samuel Johnson. But, by 1775, that great Scottish philosopher, David Hume, began to hae his doots about the authenticity of this particular piece of folklore. A few years earlier, Hume had praised Macpherson and referred to him as 'the Scottish Homer' but he now declared, 'If fifty bare-arsed Highlanders should say that 'Fingal' was an ancient poem, I would not believe them!'

Daft Auld Scots and Gaelic Proverbs

! Life consists in not breathing but enjoying life

! *Aithnichear an leomhan air scriob de iongann –*
The lion is known by the scratch of his claw

! *Am fear a bhios fadaig an aiseig, Gheibh e thairis uaireigin –*
He that waits long at the ferry will get across sometime

! As wanton as a wet hen

! *Is fhearr duine na daoine –*
A man is better than men

! *An truir nach fuiling an cniodachadh, Seann bhean, cearc, agus caora –*
Three that won't bear caressing, an old woman, a hen and a sheep

! Nipping and scarting is Scotch folk's wooing

! He that's born to be hanged will never be drowned

! *Bithidh na gabhair bodhair 's an fhogar* –
The goats will be deaf at harvest time

! Drunk folk seldom take harm

! *Is labhrach na builg fàs* –
Empty bladders are loquacious

! *Cha sheas càirdeas air a lèth-chois* –
Friendship will not stand on one leg

! *A cram'd kyte maks a crazy carcase*

! A daft nurse maks a wise wean

! *Phòs mi luid air son a cuid, Dh fhalbh a cuid is dh'fhan an luid*
I married a trollop for her gear, her gear has gone, but
she's still here

! *Làmh fhad, is cead a sìneadh* –
A long arm and leave to stretch it

! Be lang sick that ye may be soon well

! A midge is as big as a mountain, amaist

Two points worth making about the above. For every silly
saying in the Scots and Gaelic traditional canon, there are a
dozen wise ones. And just to show that we're not the only
nation that gets hung up on occasionally bizarre proverbial
advice, check out the following popular sayings from around
the world:

! Dry pants catch no fish (Bulgaria)

! There's no economy in going to bed to save candles if the
result be twins (China)

! Mistakes ain't haystacks or there'd be more fat ponies
than there is (Midwest US of A)

The Glory Days

Up until quite recently, there has been much bleating about the number of foreign footballers making their livings in Scotland – and damaging the prospects of our up and coming youngsters. However, you must pity the poor old English in the late 1800s when soccer south of the Border was inundated with Scottish talent; the 'Scotch professors' as they were known.

In 1892, the first Liverpool team was made up entirely of Scots. As football historian Bill Murray has so acutely observed, 'In the 1870s, the money was in England and the talent in Scotland.' Some of us still believe that!

It is also true that Scots were instrumental in getting football up and running in England. Lord Arthur Kinnaird, who was born in 1847 at Rossie Priory, Inchture, Perthshire, learned his football at Eton and went on to become a pioneering administrator with the Football Association. He was no slouch on the park, captaining Old Etonians in the 1883 FA Cup Final. He was known for his 'robust' style of play and it was his wife who expressed the fear that one day he might come home with a broken leg. A friend, who had often seen Arthur play, reassured her that, if he did, it wouldn't be his own.

The Tight-Arsed Hammer of the Scots

King Edward I of England, no great admired of Scotland or the Scots, graphically if crudely spelled out his achievement when, after the military campaign in 1296, he broke the nation's Great Seal and pinched our national treasures such as the Stone of Destiny. He declared, 'A man does good business when he rids himself of a turd.'

Munros, Corbetts and . . . Hewitsons

Now, don't talk to me about mountains. As the original couch tattie, I avoid hills whenever I can, regarding them as one of God's glorious, but great, mistakes. The Munros, of course, are Scotland's 284 mountains over 3000 feet and Corbetts are the wee pimples that soar to a mediocre height of between 2500 and 3000 feet. There are said to be 221 of the latter.

We all must know somebody who is a Munro- or Corbett-bagger. They have a little list that they tick off after a weekend on the hills and smile that self-satisfied smile. And they'll turn you into senseless stone in the pub recounting the famous day they did twenty Munros in a day, in the teeth of a force-nine gale and with a badly sprained ankle.

Now, for the vast majority of us who find it difficult to climb the stairs to bed at night, never mind dragging ourselves up a mountain, I can now offer the 'Hewitsons', veritable molehills alongside the Munros and Corbetts but the high-lights of my climbing life. The greatest delight is that there are only three of them and, although rather spread across the land, they should restore the confidence of anyone intimidated by the Munro-baggers or the Corbett-crunchers:

	KILBOWIE HILL CLYDEBANK	BERWICK LAW EAST LOTHIAN	BEN BHRAGGIE CAITHNESS
HEIGHT	400 feet	300 feet	1246 feet
SURFACE	Concrete	Dog-walkers path	Moor track
REASON CLIMBED	Missed last bus	Forced by my children	Forced by my parents
REWARDS AT TOP	Pubs	Crackin' whale's jawbone	Statue of Chookie Sutherland
VIEW	Post-industrial	Rural	All the way to the Red River

The Taking of Dumbarton Rock

In an age that regards scrambling over mountains, throwing yourself off bridges or scaling sheer cliffs as fun, it's easy to underestimate the achievement of Captain Thomas Crawford of Jordanhill who led a daring climb up Dumbarton Rock in 1571 to take the castle for Mary, Queen of Scots. It was an epic escapade. As if he didn't have enough problems, as they humphed ladders, grappling hooks and assorted weapons up the cliff face, one of his troops suffered what historians suggest was an epileptic fit. He was lashed to the ladder, which was turned to the rock face, allowing the assault team to climb past unhindered.

Morag's Magical Scottish Kitchen
CARRAGEEN JELLY

1 large bag of seaweed
1 quart milk

First gather your seaweed. It is important to take it from rocks that are washed by the tide and not from along the high tide line. Wash all the salt and sand out of the seaweed and spread it on a cloth out-of-doors to dry and bleach for several days. (Pray for several dry days at this stage.)

When it is thoroughly dry, put it in a pillowcase and hang it up in a warmish place.

As and when required, stir two dessertspoons of your dried seaweed into a quart of milk. Simmer until the milk begins to thicken. Strain the milk and seaweed mixture into a bowl and leave it to cool and set.

(An acquired taste!)

Saved by the Balefire

In 1716, the retreating Jacobite army operated a scorched earth policy and among the communities to suffer was Dunning in Perthshire where all but one of the thirty-five houses are said to have been burned down. The surviving cottage was saved by the quick-thinking owner who lit a bale of straw in his front room. The Jacobites, seeing the plumes of smoke, passed by thinking the house was already well alight.

Hard-Boiled and Thick-Skinned

The world is too much with us of late. In my youth, in a simpler, slower, less demanding world, the highlight of the week was a guid Scots boiled egg – done to a T, with a runny yolk wrapped in a firm white casing and taking precisely three minutes to reach this state of perfection.

Nowadays, I find it takes nearly twice that time. The reason, I'm told by my farmer friends, is that a change in feedstuffs for the hens has led to them laying eggs with thicker, more heat-resistant shells. But here's a tip – adding a tablespoon of sugar to the boiling water can reduce the required boiling time by up to a minute.

Chic Murray, who appears in greater depth elsewhere in this miscellany, tells of a visit to the doctor who informed him he had only three minutes to live. On receiving this 'terrible news', Chic says, 'I immediately asked if there was anything he could do for me.'

His doctor replied, 'Well, I could boil you an egg.'

Six Devious Disguises

The Masked Preacher

Masked, like the Lone Ranger, Covenanting minister, the Rev. Alexander Peden from Ayrshire, rode the countryside in the 1660s preaching at illegal open-air services or conventicles. Peden went one better than the masked cowboy and also wore a wig. His disguise is now in the possession of the National Museum of Scotland.

The Tartan Army c. 1150

An abbot of Bury St Edmonds described how, in the second half of the twelfth century, he undertook a dangerous business trip to Rome, along the much-trod pilgrim routes through France and Italy. To avoid detection, he kitted himself out in the ragged gear of the typical Scot, walking barefoot with his shoes slung over his shoulder. To give that added touch of authenticity, when he was approached, he shook his walking stick and cursed in 'the threatening manner of the Scots'.

Chip off the Old Block

Bonnie Prince Charlie, who famously dressed up as Flora MacDonald's maid Betty Burke to evade capture after Culloden, may have learned the art of disguise from his father, the Auld Pretender, James VIII. On his way to the 1715 Jacobite uprising, he crossed France dressed as a priest.

Attack of the Killer Cows

Masquerading as cattle, in long, dark frocks, an SAS-style squad under the Earl of Douglas were able to get to the foot of the battlements at the previously impregnable castle of Roxburgh, then scale the walls, overwhelming the garrison and wresting the strategic fort from English control. The attack took place in February 1314 and was a major psychological victory for the Scots freedom fighters. Their disguise was so convincing apparently that two sentries patrolling the ramparts were heard by the raiders speculating on how the farmer had allowed his beasts to stray so far.

Maria Breaks the Mould

The Scottish shipyards of the industrial revolution were off-limits to women but, in the 1860s, Maria Campbell from Renfrew disguised herself as a man to get a job among the hammers' ding-dongs and worked in the yards for years, even living in the working men's hostel. Her gender deceit was discovered after she was taken to hospital suffering from smallpox.

His Lordship's on the Wagon

After the Battle of Langside in May 1568, a supporter of the defeated Mary, Queen of Scots, the noble Lord Seton, escaped to Flanders where, to earn a living, he became a wagon driver. On his return to Scotland, he recalled, with pride, those hard days at the bullock's rear end and even had his portrait painted in the garb of a wagoner.

Morag's Magical Scottish Kitchen
COLCANNON

1¹/₂ lb green cabbage, quartered	1 lb potatoes, peeled
2 small leeks	7 fl.oz milk or single cream
a pinch of ground mace	salt and freshly ground pepper
2 oz butter, melted	

Cook the cabbage in boiling salted water, until just tender, and drain.

Cook the potatoes in boiling salted water, until tender, then drain well. Mash and keep hot.

Simmer the leeks in the milk or cream until tender.

Add the leeks to the mashed potatoes and beat until smooth. Shred the cabbage and add it to potato and leek mixture. Mix everything together and put the pan over low heat, beating until it is fluffy and piping hot.

Season with the mace and salt and pepper. Pile the colcannon into a heated serving dish, make a well in the centre of it and pour in the melted butter.

(Mmmmmm!)

A Tidy Mind

One of the lesser known works of Sir Walter Scott, the world's first historical novelist and the man gets most of the blame for Scotland's bagpipes and heather persona, is the thesis he presented on joining the brotherhood of advocates. It was entitled *On the Disposal of the Bodies of Executed Criminals*.

Guarding the Secret

The tiny and increasingly rare wild Scottish primrose, the *primula Scotica*, a dark purple flower with a pale yellow eye and growing to a height of no more than 5cm, is thought to have survived through the last Ice Age (ended c. 12,000 years ago) by growing in small, ice-free refuges. Ninety per cent of the world population of this delicate wee flower, some 22,000 plants, are to be found on the far-flung Orkney island of Papa Westray, my home for twenty years. The primula usually flowers twice during the short Orkney summer and the location of the Papay colony is kept a closely guarded secret in the community. Anyone breaching the code of silence is either tied to a tidal reef and pecked by the bonxies (great skuas) or is forced eat spoots (razor fish) in a hot curry sauce.

Build Your Own Scottish Anthem

So much debate has taken place in the past few years on the merits of our national anthem – should it be 'Flower of Scotland' or 'Scots Wha' Hae' or 'The Wee Cock Sparra'? – that I feel it's time we offered a solution. The beauty of what follows is that – with suitable lubrication – it can be sung to any damn tune you fancy!

> *From such surreal scenes, auld Scotia's*
> *grandeur surely springs!!*

So, if you've got your tune ready, start with line one of your choice, add line two and so on . . .

Walking through . . .

1	2
The mean streets of Ratho	At Hallowe'en
The Scottish Parliament	During the Edinburgh Festival
The boys gate at Firhill	Four weeks into the season
Buchanan Street bus station	Looking for a friendly face
Red light district of Forfar	In the middle of a doonpour
University of Abertay refectory	On the last day of the Open Golf
The Clyde Tunnel	On my wan guid leg
The bistros of Stornoway	Oan a promise
A fish processing plant at Scalloway	Hunting for a lavvy
The fourth green at Gleneagles	Desperate for a lamb boona
The Orange Parade at Bellshill	Trying tae catch the '42' bus
Tesco's car park	Attempting to sober up

each wearing . . .	**and waving a . . . 6, shaped like a Saltire**
5	6
A mauve, suede philibeg	Haddock supper
Their mither's bloomers	Didgeredoo
A threadbare tammy	Monster haggis
A charity shop outfit	Pokey hat
Our patience a bit thin	Copy of the Declaration of Arbroath
A pair of Billy's banana boots	An Oddbin's kerry-oot
A look of misty patriotism	Bottle of Evian water
A Rab C Nesbit simmet	Traffic cone
A wet suit and flippers	Masonic apron
A tartan fru-fru	Copy of *Scottish Field*
A self-satisfied grin	Shortbread tin
Their Sunday best	Season ticket for East Stirling

It would have . . .	**to hear them . . .**
7	8
Given you the dry boke	Greet symbolically in their beer
Brought you out in a cold sweat	Tunelessly sing 'Flower of Scotland'
Sent your heartstrings twanging	Analyse the nature of Scots identity
Forced you to have a lie down	Toast the Auld Alliance
Set you looking for a dying cat	Recite 'Tam O'Shanter'
Made you apply for English citizenship	Discuss the greyhound results
Brought a tear to a glass eye	Lavish praise on Aberdeen FC
Made you tak' to the drink	Recall the days of Glasgow trams
Made you forget to buy your lottery tickets	Boast of their socialist origins
Been enough to start a riot	Do their Chick Young impersonation
Get out your old football programmes	Criticise pushy American tourists
Caused you to question your sanity	Eulogise the Blair/Bush double act

I spotted . . .

3

Martin O'Neill

Jack McConnell

Gordon Ramsay

The ghost of Robert Bruce

Aly Bain

Sean Connery's milkman

Irvine Welsh

Darius

Robbie Shepherd

The cast of *River City*

Shotts & Dykehead Pipe Band

Jimmie Macgregor

and . . .

4

Sheena Wellington

Sidney Devine

Tam Cowan

Doddie Weir

Jackie Bird

Cameron Stout

Robbie the Pict

Tommy Sheridan

Edwin Morgan

Lulu

Andrew Neil

Chic Charnley

Build Your Own Scottish Anthem

and . . .

9

Swear allegiance to the Queen.

Badmouth Jacques Chirac.

Open Another Bottle of Plonk.

Share a packet of smoky bacon crisps.

Pass round the shortbread.

Talk about emigrating.

Boast of their Scottish identity.

Plan renovation of their West End mews.

Laugh at the cost of the new Parliament.

Discuss Bertie Vogts ancestry.

Whinge over the Land Reform Act.

Scan the *Daily Record* racing section.

Doon the Dunny

The Glasgow Underground was opened in 1896.

The designer and senior engineer was Alexander Simpson.

It was the third such system in the world after London and Budapest.

On the opening day the fare was one penny.

It was so popular that thousands went round and round and officials had to intervene.

Sceptical Glaswegians fully expected the city to fall into the newly-dug tunnels.

It was cable-drawn until 1935 when it was electrified.

By the 1950s the system was carrying 36 million people every year.

The popular nickname for the system today is 'The Clockwork Orange'.

A wandering Labrador dog once brought the entire system to a halt.

The subway has its very own ghost – the Grey Lady – thought to be the spirit of a woman killed on the tracks in the 1950s.

The system is currently run by Strathclyde Passenger Transport Executive and directly employs 365 people.

The distinctive musty smell has been captured in the subway display at the city's transport museum.

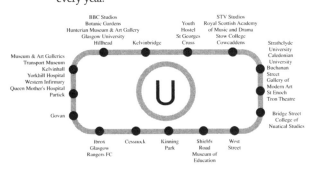

Currying Favour with the Scots

Most scholars identify the eighteenth century as the period when the Scots were first exposed to the delights of curry, the earliest recipe, having been traced to Dumfriesshire, uses spices brought back to Scotland by East India Company traders. However, there is a suggestion of earlier skirmishes with hot foods that date back to medieval Scotland. In the thirteenth century, huge quantities of spices were used in cooking at the court of Alexander III. One chronicler describes the dishes as burning with wildfire.

Despite such gourmet delights as Mars Bar suppers, a million and one varieties of pizza, kebabs by the cartload, Chinese, Malay and Thai delicacies and, of course, the classic fish supper (now requiring an extension to your mortgage to purchase), the curry is, without question, Scotland's current national dish in terms of popularity.

I like to think that Robbie Burns would have been a vindaloo man. And Bonnie Prince Charlie? Perhaps a lamb korma.

The first Scottish curry recipe is attributed to Stephana Malcolm of Langholm. She called her speciality 'Chicken Topperfield' and it dates from 1791.

In the 1950s, curry and singer Ruby Murray took off simultaneously in Scotland and the rhyming slang, that has safely stood the test of time, was born. Anyone for a Ruby?

Scottish curries are generally held to be amongst the hottest in the world and certainly out-zing anything the seedbed of India can offer. In fact, chicken tikka masala is said to have been developed in Glasgow and is now exported to India.

The Top Ten Most Obscure Clan Mottoes

CLAN	HOME GROUND	MOTTO
Douglas	Borders	'Never Behind'
Kennedy	Carrick and Galloway	'Consider the End'
MacKenzie	Kintail/Ross-shire	'I Shine, Not Burn'
MacDonald	Western Isles/Highlands	'By Sea and By Land'
Bruce	Annandale, Nithsdale	'I Have Been'
Davidson	Badenoch	'Wisely if Sincerely'
Buchanan	Loch Lomondside	'Hence the Brighter Honour'
MacIntosh	Badenoch and Lochaber	'Touch Not the Cat'
Menzies	Atholl and Strathtay	'Will God, I Shall'
Fergusson	Argyll, Dumfries	'Sweeter after Difficulty'
MacEwan	Argyllshire	'I Grow Green'

The Old Bodhisattva of Lochnagar?

Sir Hugh Rankin (1899–1988), a notorious heidbanger, riveter's mate, runner-up in the all-Britain sheep-judging competition and all-round eccentric, became a Buddhist and was convinced of the existence of abominable snowmen. He believed they were the Five Perfected Men (Bodhisattvas) who guide the destiny of the world and who meet annually either in a drafty Himalayan cave or a plush penthouse suite overlooking Caesar's Palace in Las Vegas. Apparently, one of this chosen squad normally bides in the Cairngorms.

Five Seasons in a Day

It is somehow very appropriate that Scotland, a nation that, on the weather front, can offer you four or more seasons in an hour, never mind a day, should have been the home ground of the man who is generally recognised as the first weather forecaster.

Alexander Buchan (1829–1907) from the village of Kinnesswood, just east of Kinross, began his working life as a teacher but had a passion for the weather, making his name with a paper titled 'The Mean Pressure of the Atmosphere and the Prevailing Winds of the Globe'. He became secretary of the Scottish Meteorological Society and mapped the isobars and isotherms of the world. Buchan gets the credit for discovering the fact that European weather is dictated by pressure conditions over Iceland.

He also developed a theory, having examined mountains of statistics, that Britain's climate is subject to successive warm and cold spells falling between certain dates each year. These were known as the 'Buchan Spells', hence the phrase, which you'll hear mouthed in many a pub and supermarket, football crowd and bus queue to this day, 'This is some Buchan Spell of weather we're having!'

The most prominent of the cold weather periods is in April, the so-called 'Borrowing Days'. For those whose lives are not yet crammed to overflowing with vital information the Buchan Spells are:

1st Cold Period: February 7–10
2nd Cold Period: April 11–14
3rd Cold Period: May 9–14
4th Cold Period: June 29–July 4
1st Warm Period: July 12–15
5th Cold Period: August 6–11
2nd Warm Period: August 12–15
6th Cold Period: November 6–12
3rd Warm Period: December 3–9

Some Scottish Weather Stats

November to February is the mistiest period in Scotland but, along the east coast, it is possible to get mist at any time of the year. Mist forms during a period when the temperature is decreasing. Near the coast, cool seas can allow mist to persist for days and this is known as haar

The driest town in Scotland is Arbroath with an average rainfall of just 594mm per annum

For Scotland as a whole, the wettest month is October with an average rainfall of 161.7mm

The wettest place in Scotland is Kinlochewe in Ross-shire with around 2210mm per annum. However, some areas without recording stations probably receive an annual average of over 3000mm

The strongest gust on record for Scotland was on Cairngorm Summit, on 20 March, 1986, when a wind speed of 173mph was recorded

At low level, the windiest place in Scotland is Fair Isle, Shetland, with an annual mean speed of 20.6mph

The lowest ever temperature in Scotland is -27.2°C. It was recorded at Braemar, Aberdeenshire, in January 1982

The hottest summers were 1933 and 1976 – both with a mean temperature of 16.5°C

The highest ever temperature in Scotland is 32.8°C which was recorded twice at Dumfries in July 1901 and July 1908

Over the centuries the island of Tiree, in the Inner Hebrides, has emerged as a location of remarkable climatic extremes. It claims to be the sunniest place in Scotland but is also the windiest with the highest average of 100mph gusts

The West of Scotland can often seem like the wettest place on the planet but it's an unusual fact that there are more palm trees in Argyll than in any other county in the British Isles

The most rain in a single day fell at Loch Sloy, by Loch Lomond, on 17 January 1974 when 238mm was recorded. Astonishingly this is almost half Arbroath's annual rainfall

The strongest gust of wind ever recorded in Scotland at low level was 142mph at Fraserburgh on 13 February 1989

Knox Mist His Calling

Interestingly, we have a record of John Knox as a weather reporter. When Mary, Queen of Scots arrived at Leith from France at 7 a.m. on the dull, overcast morning of 19 August 1561, to take the reins of government, John Knox wrote:

The very face of heaven, the time of her arrival, did manifestly speak what comfort was brought unto this country with her; to wit, sorrow, dolour, darkness and all impiety; for in the memory of man, that day of the year, was never seen a more dolorous face of the heaven, than was at her arrival, which two days after did so continue; for beside the surface weet and corruption of the air, the mist was so thick and so dark, that scarce might any man espy ane other the length of two butts. The sun was not seen to shine two days before nor two days after. That forewarning God gave unto us; but, alas, the most part were blind.

Yeah, Blame the Sunshine

In 1937, the lodger in a Glasgow house appeared in court and confessed to having brought back more than a suntan from his years of exile in the United States. The man was convicted of breach of the peace but told the court in mitigation that he had suffered from sunstroke while living in California and whenever he took a drink it did strange things to his head. Yeah, we know.

Wind in His Sails

Fifer Sir William Reid, who was born at Kinglassie, Fife, in 1791, was a leading nineteenth-century expert on gales and storms, By a nice twist of fate, Sir William was, for a time, the Governor of the Windward Isles.

Morag's Magical Scottish Kitchen
Beremeal Bannocks

4 oz plain flour

2 heaped tsp baking soda

12 oz beremeal

2 oz butter

1 tsp salt

1 heaped tbsp cream of tartar

1 pint buttermilk

Sieve the flour, salt, baking soda and cream of tartar together into a mixing bowl. Add the beremeal and mix. Rub in butter and then mix in the buttermilk to make a soft dough.

Heat a lightly greased girdle until it is hot. Cook the bannocks for about 2–3 minutes on each side.

The bannocks can be served warm or cold and they are delicious with Orkney cheese or with a traditional fry-up.

(This is what put the bannock in Bannockburn!!)

Sturdy Beggars over the Centuries

If you thought public concern about aggressive begging on the city streets of Scotland was something new, think again. In 1579, beggars, minstrels, fortune-tellers, vagrants, idle rogues and 'vagabond scholars' (don't look at me in that tone of voice!) in Aberdeen, Glasgow and St Andrews had their activities outlawed by an act emanating from the Scots Parliament. In 1616, Edinburgh acted independently to rid itself of the tribes of beggars who were infesting the town and passing their time 'in all kind of riot and filthy lechery'.

Vagrants and strolling beggars were causing increasing anxiety in Dumfries in 1809 and licences were issued allowing them to beg in neighbouring parishes. In 1832, beggars flooding in from country districts were causing concern to Glasgow magistrates. Less than twenty years later, in Glasgow, street begging was reported to be very prevalent with 'stout, young idle women and girls' loitering in the main thorough-fares, with children in their arms.

Today the homeless street beggar, huddled under a blanket, hand outstretched, is a commonplace sight, particularly for city folk going home to a warm fire and a laden table, but the realisation that this underclass still exists is sobering.

Mind you, more people might be inclined to give if the begging was less 'in yer face' and, to be brutally honest, the street beggars of Scotland don't do themselves any favours. Generally, they greet you warmly enough even if you aren't dipping into your pocket but just occasionally you come across one of the fraternity who lets the side down.

An acquaintance was accosted in Dundee by a lean and hungry-looking chiel who asked for money for a sandwich. My friend, on her break from the office, had no cash with her but, rather generously, I thought, offered him the pre-packed sandwich she had just bought. He took the pack, inspected it carefully and handed it back, declaring, with a candour that left my friend gob-smacked, 'Ah dinna like cheese and onion – is that all you've got?'

Following exhaustive research throughout the land, in many a doorway and pedestrian underpass, I now offer you the most common responses that people, reluctant to part with a few bob, offer to street beggars:

Nae chance, pal!

Ah'll miss ma bus.

Will you take a cheque?

Ah've already given to the chap in the next doorway.

Ah've broke ma wrist.

Get a joab!!

Sorry, chief, Ah'm deef.

Ah'll see you a'right next time.

My ma's got a blanket like that.

Ma granny has gone into labour.

Sorry, Ah'm a student – does this pay well?

If you detect a touch of class bias in some of these answers, then you're spot on. But I have to say that the general impression of our street beggars is that the Scots – even in Aberdeen – are a generous and sympathetic crew (barring the customary Friday night louts) and that they would rather beg here than in the back streets of Baghdad.

My top man in the streets of Aberdeen is Smiler Craig. His winning grin is his umbrella against the storms of life and he is famed along Union Street. Recently he was the recipient of some homespun wisdom from an elderly female passer-by. He greeted the woman and, as she dropped fifty pence into his bunnet, she told him, 'That smile may warm other people's hearts, son, but it'll no' keep the cold out o' yours.'

Morag's Magical Scottish Kitchen

CRANACHAN

1 oz caster sugar
2 tbsp water
1 oz pinhead oatmeal
10 fl.oz double cream
1 tbsp whisky
1 tbsp heather honey
3½ oz Scottish raspberries
4 sprigs of mint to garnish

Caramelised oatmeal is the key to a successful cranachan. Put the caster sugar and a tablespoon of water in a small pan on a low heat, until the sugar melts, then turn up the heat and boil the mixture until it turns a rich caramel colour like dark, runny, honey. Do not stir!

Toast the pinhead oatmeal in frying pan over a medium heat – swirl round pan constantly in order that it browns evenly.

When the sugar syrup is ready, quickly add the toasted oatmeal to it, stir and then pour on to a sheet of baking parchment and leave it to cool. When the mixture has set, remove it from the parchment and pound it until it resembles salt crystals. (This is a good job for your assistant chef!)

Whip the cream until it forms soft peaks. Add the pounded oatmeal mixture to the whipped cream, then stir in the whisky and honey. Carefully incorporate the raspberries, keeping twelve back for decoration. Spoon the cranachan into four glasses and decorate each with three (not four) raspberries and a sprig of mint.

Pies for the Boys

A cod's head pie, devised by Isabella Elder, wife of the Glasgow shipbuilder John Elder, became internationally famed as a cheap, palatable and nutritious meal that was ideal for working men. The dish achieved fame in a very roundabout manner, having been mentioned in dispatches by the US ambassador in the 1880s.

Around the same time, Nellfield Pies became an Aberdeen legend. It was discovered that an over-enthusiastic supervisor at the city's Nellfield Cemetery routinely exhumed and destroyed corpses to make way for new burials. He also happened to be a baker and the story, à la Sweeney Todd, soon grew wings.

The Precedence Quiz

Okay, in this egalitarian world, it may seem outmoded, even absurd, that one human being should have officially-sanctioned precedence over another. But it happens. You'll hear it said that, without such systems, society would fall apart. I wonder.

Hidden away in a dusty vault, I've discovered the offishul Scottish list of precedence, established and fine-tuned over the centuries and ranging over dozens of categories from top nobs to mere 'gentlemen' – but no 'gentlewomen', you'll note.

I've found a report, dating back to 1568, of an inquiry into the bad blood between Dundee and Perth caused by the dispute over which of the two towns should get precedence after Edinburgh in the annual Riding of the Three Estates. So it's not just a footballing rivalry between St Johnstone and Dundee – the animosity between the clubs actually has a long pedigree.

Here's a wee test to help you negotiate this social minefield, save you embarrassment and ensure that you know your place in this confusing world. Answers below.

Questions

1. You are the Lord Advocate and you're waiting in the queue in a burger bar, in Union Street, Aberdeen, for your triple cheeseburger and fries when in walks the Secretary of State for Scotland (Remember, though, it's not the job it used to be!). Do you have precedence?

2. You are the Moderator of the General Assembly of Scotland queuing to see Westlife live in the Virgin Megastore, in Argyle Street, Glasgow, when in walks the Keeper of the Great Seal (Keep a straight face at the back there!). Do you have to give way?

3. You are the Chookie Argyll standing in line at the UGC in Dundee to see the new *Matrix Overloaded* movie when in walks the Duke of Norfolk. Do you stand aside?

4. You are the Sovereign joining the throng to get in to the Military Tattoo on the esplanade of Edinburgh Castle when in walks the Lord Lyon King of Arms. Do you defer?

Answers

1. Of course you don't – the Scots Secretary is still right up there in the precedence Top Twenty.

2. This is a close run thing but the Moderator has it by a sexy shoe buckle.

3. Scandalously (at least to my mind), the English duke has precedence.

4. The Sovereign is, of course, numero uno – hesitate and you're off to the Bloody Tower.

Score Assessments

1 correct: Watch your step or the executioner's block will beckon.
2 correct: Your chances of getting invited to Balmoral are pretty slim.
3 correct: You're heading up that social ladder at a rate of knots.
4 correct: Your tickets to the next royal garden party are in the post.

Defiant to the End

When, in April 1747, the Jacobite Simon Fraser, Lord Lovat (who, as an old colleague Alastair Phillips once remarked, was no role model for anyone) was being driven to the scaffold through a hostile London mob, some hacket bint in the gutter apparently yelled, 'They are going to cut your head off you ugly old Scotch dog.' To which Lovat replied disdainfully looking down his nose at the unwashed throng, 'I verily believe they are, you ugly old English bitch.'

There was clearly a common, confident trait among those Jacobite nobs. After hearing a death sentence passed on him for his role in the 1745 Jacobite uprising, Lord Balmerino, a captive from Culloden, had his coach stopped at Charing Cross on the journey to the Tower of London, so that he could purchase a pound of gooseberries.

Purposeful Pish [No. 2]

Sniffed a deerstalker lately? Well, if so, you'll be wondering, as I did for so many years, how the manufacturers of Harris Tweed managed to get the distinctive aroma – redolent of old men, bracken braes and scabby sheep – that is the hallmark of this particular type of cloth. Crotal, a type of Scottish lichen, was used to dye the wool and, by tradition, it was mixed with urine – human or animal or a mixture of both – which acts as a fixing agent and left to soak in a barrel of this mixture for about three weeks.

The unique smell is the result of a chemical reaction between the urine, wool and lichen.

Those Rebellious Scots!

That infamous, anachronistic, last verse of 'God Save the Queen', which badmouths the Scots, branding us all as rebels and troublemakers, has, for some reason, never been excised from the British anthem and can still, apparently, be used on rare occasions when the anthem is sung as a hymn.

Okay, we know that it was really a dig at the Jacobites, the hairy-arsed Highlanders of the Forty-Five uprising who didn't wash enough and dared to question good old Lowland values. However, the mere existence, 260 years on, of these lines is a kick in crutch to anyone who believes that Scotland is a place apart and not just a northern English county. Just to remind you, the offending lines run:

> Lord grant that Marshall Wade,
> May, by thy mighty aid,
> Victory bring.
> May he sedition hush,
> And like a torrent rush,
> Rebellious Scots to crush,
> God save the King.

Now, we must never forget the context of this outpouring of anti-Scottish invective. The anthem was said to have been composed by a gent called Thomas Arne. It suddenly became the song of the moment when it was performed, in the presence of George II, at the Drury Lane Theatre, in London in 1745, as the Jacobite army approached Derby.

Interestingly, another suggestion I've come across recently is that the anthem was, in fact, originally a secret Jacobite composition, written around 1715 by an Irishman called Henry Carey to welcome James VIII, the Auld Pretender, back to Scotland. The words ran along the lines of:

God save great James our King,
Send him victorious,
Soon to reign over us . . .

Whatever the true provenance (and it's not often that political correctness carries any sort of appeal for me), this offending last verse should be excised or, in the patois, given the bum's rush. We don't want anything elaborate to mark its passing but, following past practice, the most appropriate symbolic action would be to carry a copy of the offending verse, amid a vast throng, up the High Street and down into the Grassmarket where it would be cursed by the clergy, spat upon by the proletarian scum and burned by the public executioner. It might form a wee addition to the New Year celebrations in Edinburgh, come to think on it.

Morag's Magical Scottish Kitchen
'Soupie' Duff

Now here's a really sensational variation of the Orkney Duff which is effectively three meals in one pot – soup, meat and pudding. This one's a genuine world-beater but it's just between you, me and the gatepost — we don't want Messrs Nairn, Rhodes, Ramsay and Oliver getting in on this. Prepare the Orkney Duff, as on p. 25 above, up to just before the cooking stage. Instead of the heat-resistant plate, put a piece of boiling beef in the large pan with water and add some chopped-up onion, carrot, turnip and potato. Now put your tied-up pudding into the pan (knot uppermost, as before) and boil for $2 \frac{1}{2}$ hours.

(Souperb!)

Swallowing the Puddock

Weird enough that we should try to inflict alternative remedies on ourselves but forcing them on the animal kingdom is another matter. An old Scottish cure for red water fever in cattle required a frog to be pushed down the beast's throat. How many times this was successfully achieved is, unsurprisingly, not recorded!

The Black Isle Bone-Setter

It's a notable fact that folk medicine has retained its appeal right into the present day. William Mackintosh of Redcastle, one of the greatest twentieth-century Scottish exponents of folk medicine who was visited by patients from home and abroad, died, aged seventy-four, in 1936. He was never known to turn away anyone suffering from displaced bones and his obituaries suggested that, if he had cared for financial gain, his skills could have made him a wealthy man. However, he always declined money.

The Home as a Sanctuary

Hamesuckin' is the wonderfully evocative old Scots legal description of an assault committed in the house of the person assaulted, to which he or she has fled for safety, or an assault by someone who goes to a person's dwelling for that specific purpose. There are some very important exemptions – assaulting a landlord in his inn, an actor in his theatre or assaults which take place in an outbuilding, shop or office. This legislation was a reflection, in the eyes of the law makers, of the home as a place of refuge.

The Lonesome Trail

There is no question about it, the Scots have a love affair with country-and-western music – a hankering after the mournful whistle of the passing freight train and the dog with no name. In the last decade, this has manifested itself in the line-dancing craze where everyone, from wee tots to great-grannies, right across Scotland trots it out with the best of them – spurs jangling and boots clicking. A few years back, a Scots professor, David Purdie, even confirmed that line dancing ('The Stomp', 'Four Corners' and the splendidly named 'Tush Push') could help combat osteoporosis by promoting suppleness.

Years ago, I used to watch the Lone Ranger at the Saturday matinee in the Empire Cinema, Clydebank. And now, researching the strange itch felt by so many Scots emigrants to America – an agitation to know what lies over the next hill – I believe I've made a connection which at least goes some way to explain this passion for Stetsons, spurs and tush-pushing. Ben Robertson, describing the Scots and their descendants in South Carolina, lyrically suggested that 'the old restlessness will stir again, like a wind rising and we have to travel. We are like that. High winds and lonesome sounds disturb us, something within us makes us go.' Now, if that wasn't ever set to music, then it damn well should have been. The truth is that Scots and Ulster Scots were early exponents of bluegrass music and, as a result, can claim a strong impact on the present-day country scene.

My own favourite country song titles are associated with the legendary Johnny Paycheck, who died in 2003 and will always be remembered for his cover of David Allan Coe's 'Take This Job and Shove It'. Some of Paycheck's own epic compositions include '(Pardon Me) I've Got Someone to Kill', 'I Drop More Than I Drink' and, my own special delight, 'If I'm Gonna Sink (I Might as Well Go To the Bottom)'. Did this man have some mystical connection with the Scots psyche? I reckon so, pardner.

Friends of mine in the country world from Bucksburn to Beith have moseyed on down to the old corral to compile, for our benefit, a top twenty (in no particular order) of the most playful titles beloved by Scots in the country-and-western corpus. Again, there is a strange fatalistic, peculiarly Scottish take on existence in many of these songs, which are all, I'm assured, as real as the tumbleweeds that blow down Main Street, Wichita, or was that Wishaw. The music is sentimental – just like us. You may have some favourite of your own – if so just sing along and be warned, there's a dod o' male chauvinism flying around this wee feature:

DON'T THE GIRLS GET PRETTIER AT CLOSING TIME?

PROP ME UP BESIDE THE JUKEBOX (IF I DIE)

EVERY TIME I ITCH, I END UP SCRATCHING YOU

YOU'RE OUT DOING WHAT I'M HERE DOING WITHOUT

DROP-KICK ME, JESUS, THROUGH THE GOALPOSTS OF LIFE

GET YOUR TONGUE OUT OF MY MOUTH 'CAUSE I'M KISSING YOU GOODBYE

I DON'T KNOW WHETHER TO KILL MYSELF OR GO BOWLING

I'D RATHER HAVE A BOTTLE IN FRONT OF ME THAN A FRONTAL LOBOTOMY

MAMA GET THE HAMMER (THERE'S A FLY ON PAPA'S HEAD)

MY WIFE RAN OFF WITH MY BEST FRIEND – AND I SURE DO MISS HIM

YOU CAN'T HAVE YOUR KATE AND EDITH TOO

IF YOU DON'T LEAVE ME ALONE, I'LL GO FIND SOMEONE ELSE WHO WILL

YOU'RE THE REASON THE KIDS ARE SO UGLY

GET YOUR BISCUITS IN THE OVEN AND YOUR BUNS IN BED

IF MY NOSE WERE FULL OF NICKELS, I'D BLOW IT ALL ON YOU

I CHANGED HER OIL, SHE CHANGED MY LIFE

I WANNA WHIP YOUR COW

I WOULDN'T TAKE HER TO A DAWG FIGHT 'CAUSE I'M SCARED SHE'D WIN

YOU WERE ONLY A SPLINTER IN MY ASS AS I SLID DOWN THE BANNISTER OF LIFE

I have not included the possibly apocryphal 'I'm so Lonesome in the Saddle Since My Horse Died' but the search for verification goes on. Yeee-haaaa.

The Stand-In Preacher Loses It

The basis of recent moves to popularise religion and bring it back to the people has been what we might call audience participation – not something which was always appreciated in the Kirk. The story is told of an elder, standing in for the absent minister, who adopted the preacher's inquisitorial style of sermon on the theme of Jonah and the whale. Determined to milk his audience, he declared, 'Now the Lord had prepared a great fish to swallow Jonah.' The elder continued, 'Now what sort of fish would it be that the Lord had sent to swallow Jonah? Was it perhaps a shark?' (Pause for effect.) 'Was it a manta?' (Another dramatic hiatus.) 'Or a barracuda?' (Further pause for effect.)

One young woman in the audience had had enough and said, 'It micht hae been a whale.'

His thunder well and truly stolen, the surrogate preacher stormed, 'It micht hae been yer erse, you interfering bitch, taking the word of the Lord oot o' the mooth o' his servant.'

The Lost City of Ardmucknish Bay

If you thought Brigadoon was our only phantom community, then you're way off the mark. Long before sheep were crossing that imaginary hump-backed bridge and couthy neighbours were meeting at the road end, there was the lost city of Beregonium or, as it is sometimes described, Selma.

Early Scottish writers, such as Hector Boece and George Buchanan in the fifteenth and sixteen centuries, were hooked on this legend and placed the town, by reference to Ptolemy's *Geography* where it first appears, in the northern approaches to Loch Etive. The actual supposed location seems to be a vitrified fort (a pile of congealed rocks formed by high temperature, for the uninitiated) on the north side of Ardmucknish Bay, at the entrance to Loch Etive and directly opposite Dunstaffnage. More correctly, it should be called *Dun Mac Uisdeachan*, which translates as the 'Fort of the Sons of Uisneach', a squad who were connected with the ancient Celtic legend of Deirdre.

Early travellers, who had been captivated by the writings of Boece and Buchanan, were convinced they could make out the remains of a smart town with pillars, paved streets and a sophisticated drainage system. More convincingly, it is conjectured that Beregonium was a seat of Pictish or Gaelic chieftains.

But the mystery remains. The noted lexicographer and philologist John Jamieson (1759–1838) scuppered the idea that the fort might have been Ptolemy's Beregonium, saying that, according to his research, the dun had never carried that name. Furthermore, the name was actually Reregonium and a closer study of Ptolemy's work placed it in Galloway. Mind you, this was an easy mistake to make when you consider that, in ancient maps, Scotland always seems to be lying, half-cut, on her side with everything you expect to be in the south in the west, and everything in the east to the south.

So, at the very beginning of the Christian era, did we have a city in the south or southwest to rival Eboracum (York), Camulodunum (Colchester) or Londinium (London)? – somewhere like the Roman city of Silchester in Hampshire that was discovered below present-day street level? If there is such a place, it was surely the Roman frontier fort of Trimontium which lies, hidden beneath the soil, at Newstead, near Melrose. Occupied for a century from around 80 AD, it may have had a population of up to 5000, including the garrison and the community which grew up to service the town economically. Archaelogists believe that Trimontium was a good old frontier town, complete with market, bars and brothels and they tell us there is evidence that the people had lifestyles which ranged from the garishly affluent to an existence of grinding poverty. Sounds like our very own twenty-first-century frontier town – Aberdeen. Perhaps you know of other hidden Scottish towns. Answers on an incised slab, please, to . . .

Morag's Magical Scottish Kitchen
Gundie
(The sweeties at last!)

1 lb brown sugar
2 oz butter
1 tsp black treacle (use golden syrup if this isn't available)
$^1/_2$ tsp flavouring, such as aniseed or cinnamon

Put the ingredients into a pan, bring them to the boil and continue to cook over a high heat for about 10 minutes. Test whether the boiling mixture is ready at regular intervals by dropping a little of it into cold water. When the sample comes from the water quite hard, the Gundie is done.

At the last minute flavour it with the aniseed or cinnamon – or, if you want Gundie that is good for a cold, then try putting in $^1/_2$ tsp horehound.

Butter a Swiss roll tin and pour in the mixture. If you can resist the temptation, give the Gundie the chance to become quite cold and hard. You will then require a hammer or flatiron to smash it into bite-size pieces.

(Scrumptious!)

Bracken — Heather's Unfashionable Wee Sister

A couple of centuries ago it would have been a routine and regular household task to re-stuff your mattress with fresh bracken fronds. The removal of bracken from your fields always increased the quality of your pasture so a million and one (slight hyperbole) uses were found for this poor relation of straw and heather.

BEDDING FOR BOTH LIVESTOCK AND PEOPLE

ASH FROM BRACKEN WAS AN EARLY STAPLE OF SCOTTISH GLASS-MAKING

BRACKEN ASH WAS ALSO A USEFUL FERTILISER FOR SPUDS AND NEEPS

BOILED WITH TALLOW, BRACKEN COULD BE MADE INTO SOAP

BRACKEN WAS SOMETIMES USE AS THATCHING — A POOR SUBSTITUTE, MIND YOU, FOR HEATHER OR STRAW

BRACKEN WAS A SOURCE OF DYE FOR CLOTHING WITH THE FRONDS GIVING A LIME-GREEN COLOUR AND THE ROOTS GIVING YELLOW

BREE, OBTAINED FROM BOILING BRACKEN ROOTS IN WATER, WAS A POPULAR REMEDY FOR RICKETS

SCATTERING BRACKEN SPORES WAS BELIEVED TO OFFER PROTECTION AGAINST WITCHES

Purposeful Pish [3]

Here, if your dare, is a seventeenth-century remedy, dreamed up by some anonymous Scottish quack, for dimness of the eyes. Take 'salt armoniak, burnd and well brayd and mix it with ye pish of a young child and therewith anoint your eyes often.' Aye, well, you first!

The Landess List

Your granny was bound to have been the custodian of some wonderful cure-all – something that baffled medical science but was efficacious beyond all common sense. My experience of these remedies is, I think, interesting. I recall a wee bloke at primary school in Clydebank who used to get beetroot pieces for a week, great big doorstops with a half-inch thick slice of beetroot, every time he caught a cold. The poor wee bugger was forced to consume the snack under the supervision of a teacher, simply because his mother believed the vegetable cleared the cold.

In my own family, my youngest daughter Katy suffered badly from chilblains as a teenager. We tried everything including an infamous Orcadian technique of plastering the tootsies with a mash of neeps and garlic. It may have given her a bit of relief but it surely wrecked her social life.

One man, who knew a thing or two about these unlikely yet wonderful cures, was the Rev. Landess of Robroyston on the outskirts of Glasgow. In 1670, he gathered together a collection of 'singular remedies'. For your delectation his main findings are presented below. It is not recommended that you try any of these at home without a safety net and a strong stomach.

Gout: Since encountering the Landess List, I've become convinced that the reverend gentleman suffered terribly from gout – he could have produced a book on gout cures alone. Here's just a couple: (1) Take a fat goose . . . stuff the belly with three of four young cats, well chopped into pieces, seasoned with a handful of bay salt, plus the skin of a vulture's foot and 20 snails (alright so far?) . . . then roast the goose and save all the dripping. This is the precious ointment. (2) Roast dog also worked well, particularly when filled with frogs and black snails; use the dripping as before.

Earache: A mix of goose grease, earthworms, garlic and saffron was, apparently, just the ticket.

Toothache: The liquid produced by boiling frogs in vinegar and the liquid obtained from certain plants which the clergyman called 'spurge' worked wonders.

Rough Cough: Beans and radish are recommended for a bad cough. From my own experience of summer Scout camps, I can certainly testify that a surfeit of beans definitely discourages violent coughing.

Ticklish Cough: Try an onion roasted under the embers of the fire with sugar candy and fresh butter. Worked a treat, we're told.

Headache: Take 'violet oyl and women's milk' (hey, steady oan!) in equal quantities, mix in a hen's egg yolk, put in a poultice and 'apply warm to the place where the payn is'.

Nosebleed: Dead simple and obvious – pour vinegar in your ear.

Itch in Children: Pish again! A handful of green mint soaked in 'old pish' for twenty-four hours until it grows tender then wash the body with the liquid.

Dry Boke: Should you experience over-vomiting, having emptied the stomach, then wash your feet with hot water.

Constipation: A safe means for 'keeping the body laxative' was to regularly take a broth made from 'mercury, mallows, leetice, beets and spurge' (the aforementioned plant milk – *see under* **Toothache**). It is recommended that this is best taken in the spring or autumn (and very close to the nearest loo, I shouldn't wonder).

Down at the Club

The so-called 'Hellfire Clubs' or 'Sulphur Societies', which flourished in Edinburgh in the 1700s, caused great concern among the God-fearing. These particular clubs offered opportunities for men of 'atheistical opinions' to meet and spark some fire and brimstone, not to mention their participation in rituals involving goats and exposed calves, all of which had ordinary souls throwing up their hands in dismay. Many different sorts of clubs flourished, during the eighteenth and early nineteenth centuries, each with their own particular idiosyncrasies. Drink was often a common factor among these get-togethers for those free-thinking individuals. The following are some of the most bizarre:

> The members of **THE ODD FELLOWS CLUB** certainly enjoyed a wee refreshment but, more interestingly, they identified themselves by writing their names upside down.

> **THE DIRTY CLUB** was not a place that offered doubtful entertainment of a sexual nature but a brotherhood where, strangely, clean clothes were forbidden.

> **THE PIOUS CLUB** was not, as you might expect from the name, a gathering of the most devout but a club which met in a pie house and, at each meeting, every member was expected to devour at least one huge crusty pie.

> **THE GAGG COLLEGE** was a Glasgow club that met in an obscure tavern in the early 1800s.

Eminent professors from the university gathered and swapped jokes in what was the nineteenth-century equivalent of today's stand-up comedy clubs.

THE CAPE CLUB was a gentleman's society founded in 1762 with all members, including the infamous Deacon Brodie, sporting long cloaks.

THE SWEATING CLUB, of the nineteenth century, was composed of a band of rogues who, after taking on a cargo of drink, pursued passers-by, jostling and pushing the victim around until the poor soul began to perspire.

THE BOAR CLUB was the haunt of fashionable young men and got its name because the club met in a tavern where the innkeeper's name was Hogg and the young gents put club 'fines' for unnamed misdemeanours in a stoneware pig.

THE LAWNMARKET CLUB's members were mainly wool traders who met, early in the morning, to exchange the gossip of the day. They would then, inevitably, adjourn to a tavern for a breakfast-time glass of brandy.

THE SPENDTHRIFT CLUB, as its name suggests, was renowned for the extravagance of its middle-class members on their nights out around the hostelries of Edinburgh.

Elephants My Speciality

Many Scots have gained their reputations through unusual aspects of scientific research. Nineteenth-century naturalist and paleontologist, Andrew Adams, who worked worldwide while serving as an army surgeon, made his name studying fossil elephants. In the 1700s, eminent Dundee physician and surgeon, Dr Patrick Blair, brought himself to prominence as an anatomist with his spectacular dissection of an elephant that had died while on a visit to Tayside.

Nowadays, groundbreaking and occasionally unusual research is mostly in the hands of our institutions of higher education. To give you an idea of the incredible range of work currently being undertaken, our agents penetrated the labs and lecture halls of our universities to report on some recent research which, although having global implications, remains, somehow, very Scottish:

> An army of sulphur-eating bacteria is to be employed in an effort to tackle the problem of the annual dumping of eighteen million used tyres throughout Britain. Scientists hope that the bacteria will convert the tyres back to reusable rubber.
>
> *(Napier University, Edinburgh)*

> Psychologists have discovered how humans not only select long-term partners who look like themselves but how women are attracted to men who look like their fathers and men are more likely to end up with women who remind them of their mothers.   *(University of St Andrews)*

> Researchers discovered that national identity remains crucially important to Scots despite globalisation and recent setbacks with the new Edinburgh Parliament. National identity is seen as being on a par with people's sense of themselves as parents.
>
> *(University of Edinburgh)*

A colour label designed to warn customers about food that is going off has been developed. Changes in the quality of the food would activate the indicator and alert stores and shoppers to any leaks in supposedly oxygen-free packs.

(University of Strathclyde)

How much is a wild goose worth? Or an unspoilt river? Or the freedom to climb mountains? Scientists are asking the public for their take on these ideas so that the taxpayers' aspirations can be built into cost-effective government policies.

(University of Glasgow)

A research centre, in the form of a games laboratory, has opened. Here students can use the latest technology to learn how to create computer games software – everything from educational games for the younger audience to complex strategy games.

(Glasgow Caledonian University)

Primate researchers have discovered that 'silverback' mountain gorillas in Rwanda have been more aggressive in recent years and that the population is thriving despite poaching, loss of habitat and civil war.

(University of Stirling)

A unique computer programme, using a character recognition system, is being developed in order to translate hieroglyphics from Egyptian buildings, monuments and artefacts into English text.

(Robert Gordon University, Aberdeen)

Research has cast doubt on assertions that anti-English prejudice is putting English people off coming to live and work in Scotland. Eighty-eight per cent of English settlers questioned said that neighbours and work colleagues had accepted them and that they had assimilated easily into their new communities.

(University of Dundee)

Scientists are looking at ways of making computers work a thousand times faster by bonding traditional silicon chips to specially developed 'opto-electronic chips' – a chip 'buttie' in fact – which can use light beams to communicate information.

(Heriot-Watt University, Edinburgh)

Scottish students are co-operating with NASA to subject crabs to microgravity in a diving plane. Their tests concentrate on the effects this has on the crustaceans' nerve cells which could one day help robots and humans work better in space.

(University of Aberdeen)

The fruit of the argan tree, which grows in temperatures of 45°C in the Moroccan desert, could contain a yeast which flourishes in extreme heat and may hold the key to making better beer, scientists think. Currently yeasts have to be cooled during the brewing process.

(University of Abertay, Dundee)

Now, if you reckon that some of these research projects are off the wall, then think again. Around the world, scientists are involved in some quite remarkable – and obscure – work. Here are some of the more bizarre examples: in Australia, they study belly-button fluff; in Japan, they've trained pigeons to discriminate between the works of Picasso and Monet; in India, scientists are calculating the surface area of Indian elephants; in Canada, of all places, a study has looked at injuries caused by falling coconuts; a pair of American boffins, from Michigan, are arguing that black holes fulfil all the technical requirements to be the location of hell; and, wouldn't you know it, the Dutch are involved in magnetic-resonance imaging of male and female genitals during coitus and female sexual arousal.

Aye, it's a hard life for thae academics!

A Pocketful of Loose Change

It used to be the sign of wild Friday night when you woke up on Saturday weighed down with loose change – not a note in sight. In medieval Scotland, when all we had were coins, maybe the only way you could tell if it had been a good night was the intensity of hammer blows in your heid. Recalling these far-off days, there follows a list of Scottish coinage that might have found its way into your pooch:

$$2 \text{ DOITS} = 1 \text{ BODLE}$$
$$2 \text{ BODLES} = 1 \text{ PLACK}$$
$$3 \text{ PLACKS} = 1 \text{ SCHILLIN}$$
$$40 \text{ PLACKS} = 1 \text{ MERK}$$
$$20 \text{ SCHILLINS} = 1 \text{ PUND}$$

In the pubs it was important to know that:

$$4 \text{ GILLS} = 1 \text{ MUTCHKIN}$$
$$2 \text{ MUTCHKINS} = 1 \text{ CHOPPIN}$$
$$2 \text{ CHOPPINS} = 1 \text{ PINT}$$
$$2 \text{ PINTS} = 1 \text{ QUART}$$

Now, repeat after me . . .

And if you had wheat, peas, beans or meal to weigh, your measure of choice would have been the lippie which was equivalent to 2.268 litres. The lippie was also used to measure barley, oats and malt but, for these, it was equal to 3.037 litres. No cause for confusion there, then.

Fabled Corners of Scotland

According to the 2001 census, the population of Scotland is 5,062,011. Whatever the number, there have always been indicators, over the centuries, that, whether we are Gaels or Scots, Borderers or Shetlanders, we are still living in each other's pockets, in tight-knit communities where everyone knows everyone else's business.

Perhaps you've heard of the concept of 'Six Degrees of Separation' which argues that anyone in the world can be connected to anyone else in just six leaps. Eerily, in Scotland, that figure might be as few as three – perhaps even two – and means that, whether you like it or not, you have a very close connection with the great and the good. Scary! For example, the father-in-law of an Orkney friend of mine used to tend Alex Salmond's garden in Linlithgow. Need I say more?

One area where this consciousness of being part of a close community is taken to unusual extremes is in Scottish literature. Only the bravest novelist would risk naming the community where his or her action is set mainly because of the danger of causing offence to the neebors and even a flurry of lawyer's letters. This has resulted in an alternative geography of Scotland with imaginary towns springing up across the map, in theory, to preserve civic anonymity. Let's have a spin aboot this 'other' Scotland of the mind and, by way of illustration, have look at a few of the towns I've encountered when reading Scottish literature.

> Hamnavoe (Stromness), in *Greenvoe* by
> George Mackay Brown
>
> Dunster (Dunbeath), in *The Silver Darlings* by
> Neil M Gunn

Kinraddie (Arbuthnott), in *Sunset Song* by
    Lewis Grassic Gibbon

Thrums (Kirriemuir), in *A Window in Thrums*
    by J M Barrie

Calderwick (Montrose), in *Imagined Corners* by
    Willa Muir

Marsh End (Markinch), in *The Edge of the Wood*
    by Alan Bold

Cadzow (Lanark), in *The Awakening of George
    Darroch* by Robin Jenkins

Barbie (Ochiltree), in *The House with the Green
    Shutters* by George Douglas Brown

Graithnock (Kilmarnock), in *Docherty* by
    William McIlvanney

Unthank (Glasgow), in *Lanark* by Alasdair
    Gray

Levenford (Dumbarton), in *Hatters Castle* by
    A J Cronin

Brieston (Tarbert), in *Gillespie* by
    John MacDougall Hay

Oceania (Jura), in *Nineteen Eighty-Four* by
    George Orwell

Great Todday (Barra), in *Whisky Galore* by
    Compton Mackenzie

Top marks in this game of displaced places must surely go to Robert Louis Stevenson who located *The Strange Case of Dr Jeykll and Mr Hyde* in some bleak city called London. But, curiously, the setting has the atmosphere, the smell, the mysterious back wynds and a terraced new town that are remarkably like Edinburgh's – just as Bob had planned.

As the Feathers Fly

Falconry centres have been springing up across the country in the past few years and it surely is a marvellous sight to see hawk and man working together in a 'sport' which reached its peak during the age of chivalry and is basically about downing unsuspecting feathered passers-by.

Now, just in case you think this all a bit 'Court-of-King-Arthur-ish' and has no relevance to modern life except as an interesting adjunct of our tourist industry, then think again, my friend. We should remember that it could, just occasionally, be the passport to fame and a wee fortune. This turned out to be the case for young William Alexander, later Earl of Stirling, whose family had a small estate near Menstrie. His chance first meeting, in the late 1500s, with James VI, who was out hawking in the Stirlingshire hills, was the spark that ignited his illustrious diplomatic and political career.

The fact that James was a real hawking enthusiast is clear from the records. In 1605, affairs of state were taking second place for James as can be seen from his correspondence with the Earls of Mar and Errol which was devoted, almost exclusively, to his concern over his favourite hawk, which had taken ill.

If it turns out that hawking regains its social cachet, then you will really have to be armed with the proper vocabulary. Here's a selection of 'must have' hawking phrases.

THE LANGUAGE OF HAWKS & DOVES

bate (*verb*)   to beat the wings fiercely   from Old French *batre* 'to beat'

gled (*noun*)   another name for the kite   from Gaelic *glede* a falcon, hawk, etc.

haggard (*noun*)   a hawk that has lived wild in its first year and is, therefore, harder to train   from French *hagard*; perhaps related to **hedge**

jesses (*pl. noun*)   short straps of leather fixed the hawk's legs   from Old French *ges*, from Latin *jucere* 'to throw'

lure (*noun*)   a dead bird used to train the hawk to sit patiently at the kill   from Old French *luere*, related to German *Luder* 'bait'

man (*verb*)   to school (a bird) from the hand   from French *main* 'hand'

seeling (*noun*)   the first step in training, during which a wild hawk is kept blind by hooding it   from Middle English *seel* 'to stitch the eyes (of a hawk) shut', from Latin *cilium* 'eyelid'

sharp (*adj*)   ravenous   from Old French *ravineus*, from *raviner* 'to ravish'

stoop (*noun*)   a controlled downward swoop of a bird to the lure   from Old English *stupian* (verb)

watch (*verb*)   to keep (a bird) alert   from Old English *waecce* 'wakefulness'

The Strain of the Pipes

Long after the post-Culloden clampdown, bagpipers still find themselves regularly under attack. A piper was fined £15 for playing illegally on Hampstead Heath in London in 1996. And, before the World Cup in France, Scottish football officials had to plead with French security chiefs for the pipes not to be classed as a dangerous weapon, which is exactly how the British government had treated them post-Culloden. Here are a few pieces of anti-piping agitprop you might find circulating in the eel parlours of Wapping:

How do you get two bagpipers to play in unison?
> *Shoot one of them.*

How many bagpipers does it take to change a light bulb?
> *Five. One to change the bulb and four others to criticise his fingering technique.*

Why do bagpipers always walk when they play?
> *A moving target is more difficult to hit.*

Pipe bands are to be found all over the world and most are splendidly named. Among my own favourites must be the New York City Department of Corrections Pipe Band, the Nae Breeks Pipe Band from New Jersey and, from Uganda, a squad that carried the fabulous title of the MacScotchers. Other notables include:

New Haven Hose Company Pipe Band, Pennsylvania
Peconic Warpipes, New York State
Highland Mist Pipe Band, Ontario
Midnight Sun Pipe Band, Yukon Territory
Chicago Stock Yard Kilty Band, Illinois
High Desert Pipes and Drums, New Mexico

Sahib Temple Pipes and Drums Corps, Florida

Mystic Highland Pipe Band, Connecticut

103rd Electricians Pipe and Drum Band Inc., Massachusetts

Rogues of Scotland, Texas

Waterworks Pub Pipes and Drums, Maine

Nutscheid Forest Pipe Band, Germany

Somme Battlefield Pipe Band, France

Onion Pipers and Drums, Germany

Happy German Bagpipers, Jade, Germany

Gdansk Pipe Band, Poland

Dalhousie Pipe Band, Switzerland

Coffs Harbour Ex-Services and Woolgoolga RSL Pipe Band, New South Wales

Sovereign Assurance City of Sails Pipe Band, Auckland

Hong Kong Heilan' Pipes and Drums

10th Singapore Boys Brigade Pipes and Drums

The above list comes with the assistance of Montie Derby in Hawaii, a man who knows his chanter from drones!

It's seldom appreciated what an important part the bagpipes played in the life of Highland communities in the eighteenth and nineteenth centuries and not just at weddings, uprisings and sic' like social events. In the north of Scotland, when the exhausting task of launching a large boat was undertaken, a piper was engaged to sweeten the toil and, by his music, encourage the 'altogether pull'. It is also on record that, in 1786, the men of Skye undertook a major road-making scheme and each squad of workers was provided with its own a piper. But, as the skirl of the pipes is swallowed up by the Celtic mist, we should note that the first mention of bagpipes north of the Border comes in the records of James IV (1473–1513) and the pipers were neither Highlanders nor Lowlanders – they were, gird yersels, Englishmen.

A Classic Scottish Utterance Internationalised

Glasgow Scots	*Jings! Crivvens! Help ma Boab!*
Catalan	*Oh déu meu! Ostres! Mare de déu*
Bavarian	*Mei o mei! Jessas, Maria und Josef! Huif ma!*
Polite Sooth	*Gosh! Help! For goodness' sake!*
Parisian Patois	*Putain! Au secours! Nomme de petit homme!*
Norwegian	*Kjaere vene! Hjelp! For Guds skild!*
German	*Ach du meine Güte! Um Gottes Willen! Hilf mir!*
Franconian	*Guder Godd! Glab di war! Hilf ma!*
Spanish	*Pobrecita! Ayuda! En el nombre del Cordero!*
Gaelic	*Obh! Obh! Mo creach! Gu sealladh orm!*
Delaware	*Kwioo! Ecei Tamwé! Wicami!*

The Beachcombers Paradise

It's an eerie, easy to remember fact that the deeply indented nature of the West of Scotland, a thousand sea lochs and a million little bays and islets (as well as a multitude of midges), gives us a huge coastline which is said to be 10,200 kilometres long, give or take a couple of rocky outcrops. This perhaps doesn't mean much until you realise that the Belgian coast is only 70 kilometres in length and, if the Scottish coasts were stretched in a straight line, that would take us almost to Kuala Lumpur, in Southeast Asia. From north to south the Scottish mainland is no more than 400 kilometres.

The Best of Scotland's Recent Road- and Trackside Art

TITLE	LOCATION	DESCRIPTION	ARTIST	DATE
Sawtooth Ramps	M8 Bathgate	**a green 'Toblerone'**	Patricia Leighton	1993
Cunothic Columns	St Enoch Underground Station, Glasgow	**huge mock hydraulic rams**	Mark Firth	1996
The Horn	M8, Polkemmet Country Park, West Lothian	**the biggest horn in Christendom**	Louise Scullion/ Matthew Dalziel	1997
Some of the People	Partick Underground, Glasgow	**travellers immortalised on an electronic billboard**	David Mach	1996
Air in Airdrie	Can't miss it!	**a giant rounda- bout lampshade**	Martine Neddam	1991
Big Heids	M8 Eurocentral, Mossend	**Easter Island in deepest Lanarkshire**	David Mach	1998

The Crazy Naming Game

DOLLY THE SHEEP (1996–2003), the first cloned animal and a product of the Roslin Institute near Edinburgh, was reproduced from a breast cell of a six-year-old ewe and was neatly named after the ample-bosomed country singer, Dolly Parton.

ROBERT III (1337–1406), King of Scots, was actually born a 'John' but memories of King John Balliol (1249–1313) were still so strong that the Scots nobility couldn't bear the thought of another King John. John had been crowned king at Scone in 1292 and many people saw him as Edward I of England's lapdog so, rather unimaginatively, the nobles opted for Robert instead. The truth is that Bob (or John) was a poor soul who wasn't up to the job of ruler and once described himself as 'the worst of kings and the most miserable of men'.

LACHLAN MACQUARIE (1761–1824) was Governor-General of New South Wales. On a final tour of Tasmania in 1821, before he returned to the UK, Lachie lost the plot and set about naming every-thing in sight – from rocks to bends in the river – after his friends, family and almost anything he could think of from back home. To this day, we still have Perth, Campbeltown, Argyle Plains, Ross Priory, Gordon Valley, Strathallan Creek, to name but a few, to remind us of this strange dubbing episode.

UTSALADY, WASHINGTON STATE is a scattered settlement in the Pacific Northwest and its name, according to the local Chinooks, means 'the place of berries'. An alternative and, some might argue, an equally romantic explanation is that a Scots frontiersman was expecting his first child. When the mother duly delivered, he shouted from his cabin window for the benefit of the whole community: 'It's a laddie! It's a laddie!' You pays yer money . . .

BRANDIE, CROMACK, HAKEY, HIMBY, GARIE were popular names for the oxen which carried out most of the work in the fields of medieval Scotland. I suspect that, 'Get a move on, ya big lazy bastard,' may also have figured.

IN THE 1300s, when French influence in Scotland was at its peak, it was all the rage, de rigueur, in fact, to adopt French names and mince up the High Street in your newly-imported sequinned codpiece, smoking a Gitanes and humming 'Je t'aime' at passing washer wives and fish gutters.

When, in 1809, plans were unveiled for a common sewer along Glasgow's Trongate, there were a few wry smiles among the populace. Contractors for the job were asked to apply to the **SUPER-INTENDENT RICHARD SMELLIE**. Experts claim that, if you are unfortunate enough to encounter a modern broken sewer, then you are 'capturing the essence' of mid Victorian Scottish cities.

The efficient chief government relief co-ordinator during the Highland Famine of 1846 was none other than the ominously named **SIR EDWARD PINE COFFIN**.

One Yarn that Doesn't Hold Water

Now I'm no' one to dispel myths. On the contrary, throughout my career, I've tried never to allow dry facts to get in the way of a good story. After all what is truth? Profundity apart, it's time to be fair to the daily newspaper of choice in the north-east, the Aberdeen *Press and Journal*, and clarify that old *Titanic* tale. As the paper's columnist Norman Harper has suggested, setting this record straight is liable to spoil a thousand after-dinner speeches – but here goes. In bringing the story of the 1912 sinking of the *Titanic* to its readership, the main news page of that local daily DID NOT, I repeat DID NOT, declare, in a banner headline, that an Aberdeen man was missing at sea and offer, as an understated sub-heading, an announcement of the great disaster. The story was, in reality, very matter of fact and tidily presented although Aberdonians wouldn't have been Aberdonians if they hadn't found room in a wee corner to make mention of the liner's 'gorgeous fittings'.

However, on a similar theme, I do have a favourite heading from the Aberdeen press. It came on August 5, 1914 when newspapers carried word of the outbreak of that most horrendous of all conflicts, World War I. Keeping things very much in perspective, on page 3, ahead of all the war news, the *Aberdeen Free Press* declaimed:

A DISAPPOINTING DAY
FORENOON OF RAINFALL AT THE TURRIFF SHOW

By the Way: How Old Is Your Toon?

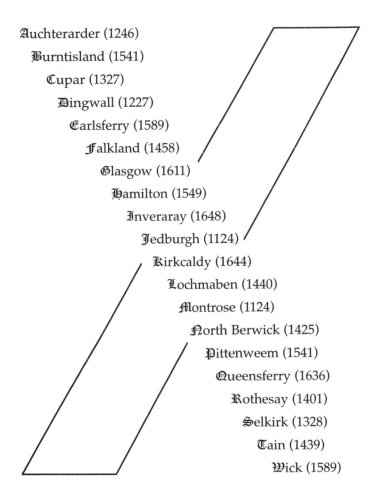

Auchterarder (1246)

Burntisland (1541)

Cupar (1327)

Dingwall (1227)

Earlsferry (1589)

Falkland (1458)

Glasgow (1611)

Hamilton (1549)

Inveraray (1648)

Jedburgh (1124)

Kirkcaldy (1644)

Lochmaben (1440)

Montrose (1124)

North Berwick (1425)

Pittenweem (1541)

Queensferry (1636)

Rothesay (1401)

Selkirk (1328)

Tain (1439)

Wick (1589)

From Sir John's Amazing Scrapbook (No. 1)

We are indebted to Sir John Sinclair (1754–1835), of Ulbster in Caithness, for more than just the introduction, to the English language, of the word 'statistics' which he is said to have poached from the Germans. He was also the man who organised and supervised *The First Statistical Account of Scotland*. It was published in 1798 and gave a remarkably detailed account of life in Scotland almost a century after the Union. It's packed with information on economics, geography and history but it also contains a good sprinkling of more offbeat folksy material.

Born at Thurso Castle in Caithness, Sinclair was the product of the Enlightenment and, frankly, he became a bit of a glutton for hard work. From the age of fifteen, he worked twelve hours a day and his writing output was truly phenomenal. He edited the entire *Statistical Account* and, in addition, wrote eighty volumes of agricultural reports and 367 pamphlets. His other claim to fame is that he was once described as the 'greatest bore' at Westminster.

The *Statistical Account* is a gold mine for any historical researcher or seeker of the obscure anecdote. For example, in the parish of Benholme in Kincardineshire, after listing those who had died from natural causes in the ten-year period 1778–88, we are given a list of the 'casualties' in the parish for the same decade. These were as follows:

DROWNED	6
SUFFOCATED	2
KILLED IN BATTLE	1
FELL FROM HORSE	1
MAD DOG'S BITE	1
FELL INTO THE FIRE	1

No sleepy backwater Benholme by the sound of that!

From Sir John's Amazing Scrapbook (No. 2)

In the late eighteenth century, tea was still an expensive luxury for most folk but the island of Stronsay in Orkney was reported to have a natural, fizzing substitute. The *Statistical Account* reported that there was a mineral spring to be found among rocks on the east coast of the islands and it was described thus:

> *The water, clear as chrystal, not unpleasant, is full of fixed air, as may be discovered by any who drink some glasses of it; for they will soon find themselves affected in the same way, as if they drank some fine brisk bottled beer.*

Lead me to it!

From Sir John's Amazing Scrapbook (No. 3)

Stress is a word that is bandied about everywhere these days but, strangely, it seems to have been missing from the records of centuries past. Did it perhaps manifest itself in other ways? Consider the description offered in the *Statistical Account* of a strange complaint called the 'Loupin' Ague'. We are told:

> *Patients have all the appearances of madness; their bodies are variously distorted; they run, when they find an opportunity, with amazing swiftness, and over dangerous passes; and, when confined to the house, they jump and climb in an astounding manner, till their strength be exhausted. Cold bathing is found to be the most effective remedy.*

Similarity to St Vitus's Dance was reported, as were

convulsive fits. Maybe these folk were just as stressed as twenty-first-century Scots – the difference being that they knew how to get it out of their systems.

From Sir John's Amazing Scrapbook (No. 4)

The wild chrysanthemum, know as 'gool', spread over large areas of Scotland in the seventeenth and eighteenth centuries and proved almost impossible to eradicate. The *Statistical Account* found traces of a system of 'Gool Courts' whose remit was to fine tenants who permitted even a single head of 'gool' to pollute their fields. In Dumfriess-shire, Sir William Grierson held such a court and fined farmers in whose growing crop three or more heads of 'gool' were discovered. And, in Perthshire, a fine of $^3/_4$d or a sheep was the penalty for a similar offence. It's even recorded that 'Gool Riders' were appointed to scour the fields, looking for chrysanthemums.

From Sir John's Amazing Scrapbook (No. 5)

There are some real gems in the *Statistical Account* relating to Orkney – presumably because of its remoteness from the mainstream life of Scotland. We learn that one parish boasted two fiddlers and a piper and the bagpiper professed, by means of his music, to be able to banish rats from their habitations with a suitable pibroch. In the parish of Orphir we find what is surely the islands' stereotype of the man of many jobs. This particular individual was beadle, sexton, cooper, slater, plasterer, boatman, gardener, kelper, mason, quarryman, labourer, thatcher and farmer. Just as an afterthought, we are told that he was the most famous begetter of male children in the parish. You wonder when he found the time.

A Selection of Unusual Assault Weapons

A hail of lemonade bottles was thrown during a
riot in George Square, Glasgow, in 1919

*A man in Aberdeen was attacked by an assailant
wielding a seagull*

In 1304, Stirling Castle was under fire from the
most modern siege engines in Europe

*A Lanarkshire woman had a bucket of hot soapy
water poured over her because her neighbours
took objection to her poor hygiene*

A Glasgow police officer was struck by dead rat
that was thrown from a 20-storey block of
flats

*A Fife resident who threw a bottle of Domestos over
a man of the cloth was charged with 'bleach of
the priest'*

One Edinburgh victim was beaten to death with
an African tribal cosh

*Travelling fans of Stranraer FC were bombarded
with stalks of celery while at a match at Berwick
in 2003*

The Electric Pencil

In the first years of the seventeenth century, Scotland's first travel writer, Lanark-born William Lithgow, voyaged all over Europe, the Middle East and North Africa. In Jerusalem, on the eve of his departure to Egypt, he persuaded a 'reluctant old friar' to tattoo the name of his sovereign, James VI, encircled by the crowns of England and Scotland, on his right arm.

Willie showed the way but Scots these days, beyond the Loyalist enclaves at least, are a wee bit more catholic in their tattoo tastes.

In the interests of a greater understanding of our culture, our roving reporter has been touring the electric pencil salons and body piercing parlours of the land to discover which tattoos are turning Scots on these days. Here is your chart rundown with the top ten most significant body ornaments:

General Tattoos	Scottish Motifs	Body Part Pierced
1. Tribal	Thistle	Navel
2. Ancient Celtic	Lion Rampant	Nipple
3. Traditional	Plain Saltire	Eyebrow
4. Football	Piper	Tongue
5. Dragon	Eagle on Saltire	Lower Lip
6. Bio-Mechanical	Clan Emblem	Ear
7. Japanese Script	Lion on Saltire	Nose
8. Skull	'Made in Scotland'	Genitalia
9. Chinese Script	Thistle on Saltire	Upper Lip
10. Family Name	Ancient Celtic	Cheek

This extensive and expensive survey also threw up some fascinating insights into the tattoo and piercing businesses:

Women account for seventy-five per cent of all requests for thistle tattoos

Tribal tattoos were popularised by George Clooney's decorations in the movie *From Dusk Till Dawn*

Celtic decoration most often comprises knots, whorls and bands in the style found in the historic *Books of Kells* which was probably produced at Iona

The most potent Scottish phallic symbol tattoo demanded by Scotsmen is the Wallace Monument at Stirling

The general consensus is that, in the coming years, traditional tattoos, such as mermaids, anchors, roses and 'I love Mother', will all make comebacks

Scotland's most spectacular tattoo is surely the image of a fish supper impressed on the butt of a chip-shop owner

Scotland's oddest tattoo must be the one in the form of a large green spot, about the size of a tennis ball, that a customer asked to have tattooed at the base of his spine – the client said the tattoo would mark the centre of his aura

Tam the Leech — Jobs which Have Gone Forever

The medieval burghs of Scotland were busy places filled with tradesfolk whose occupations, if not their job titles, are still familiar to this day – for example, the flesher (butcher) or the baxter (baker). However, less common, these days, is the professional 'leecher' who drew people's blood, using leeches, in order to improve their health. In the records of the royal burgh of Haddington, such an individual, the splendidly named Thomas the Leech, appears in 1220. This practice persisted well into the 1700s.

Here are just some of the jobs that have become redundant over the years:

> **hecklers** – whose job was dressing flax
>
> **fordswomen** – who carried burdens, including men, across streams on their backs
>
> **English improvers** – who knew exactly how our primitive agricultural system needed to be modernised
>
> **salt wives** – who worked at the salt pans (Yes, that's why Prestonpans is called Prestonpans!)
>
> **skinners** – who dealt in furs and hides
>
> **apothecaries** – who first became chemists and then went all American and now call themselves pharmacists
>
> **barber–dentists/surgeons** – who had their lucrative sidelines of pulling teeth and amputating legs taken from them
>
> **tide waiters** – who were professional beachcombers

hucksters – who were enterprising women who
bought produce in bulk at the market place and
then sold it on at profit in smaller quantities in
their own neighbourhoods

Brewing is a particularly interesting area of employment.
The manufacture of ale was one of the few occupations where
women dominated. In an age when woman were generally
marginalized and treated as second-class citizens, the brewster
wife was often a formidable character. Ale conners, municipal
beer-tasters who confirmed prices and checked the quality of
the ales, were occasionally women. It has to be admitted that
female public executioners were a bit thin on the ground.
However, such medieval fixtures as the spaewives (fortune
tellers), cairds (travelling tinkers) and coupers (market place
wheeler-dealers) are still with us.

Fishwives and fruit sellers were notoriously hardy in a
difficult era for women. The poet William Dunbar (1460–1514)
complained that the tone of Edinburgh markets was lowered
by the 'fensum flytings of defame' (foul-mouthed barnies) of
old women selling fish and fruit. The punishment for these
vulgar vixens was a calming spell in the 'jougs' – this was an
iron collar and chain attached to a wall and the offensive one
was restrained there in the hope that it would make her mend
her ways.

In the days when all the rooms in every big house had a
roaring fire, the daily job of cleaning and setting the fires fell to
the 'ashypet' or scullery maid.

I search still for documentary evidence of the existence of
that most mystical of all Scottish professions, that of the
'sharnspinner' whose task, in the days when cow muck was
used as fuel as well as fertiliser, was to turn the cowpats as
they dried on the green.

The James Gang

There have been six Scottish monarchs of the Stuart family to hold the title of James. They ruled from 1406 to 1625 with only a wee break in the mid 1500s when Mary, Reine d'Écosse ran the show. And a fine bunch of breeders they were as you can see from their performance table below:

THE 'JAMES' GANG & THEIR REIGNS	OFFSPRING
James 1 (1406–1437)	Two sons, six daughters
James II (1437–1460)	Four sons, two daughters
James III (1460–1488)	Three sons
James IV (1488–1513)	Four sons, two daughters
James V (1513–1542)	Two sons, one daughter
James VI (1567–1625)	Three sons, four daughters

It's important to remember that many of these thirty-three little princes and princesses died in infancy and that, outside this group, a significant number of Scottish royal marriages, including that of Bonnie Prince Charlie, were barren. As to little royal bastards, the numbers will forever remain a mystery but the extent of the legitimate squad does suggest this would also be a high figure.

The most startling childbirth experience of post-Union non-Stuart monarchs was surely that of Anne who reigned from 1702 (in Scotland from 1707) until 1714. She had two sons and three daughters and her thirteen other pregnancies ended in stillbirths or miscarriages.

Slavery in Springburn

One of my favourite Springburn tales is of the visit to the Atlas Railway Engine Works by the Nizam of Hyderabad who, when he saw the workers streaming home for their dinner, shouted 'Your slaves are escaping!' Now, thanks to ex-railwayman Jimmy Brown, I know the sequel to the story. The works manager reassured the Indian dignitary, saying, 'Don't worry, they'll be back.'

And, right enough, at one o'clock, the whistle blew and the workforce trooped back in. When asked about the locomotive he wanted to buy the visitor replied, 'Never mind the engine. How much do you want for that whistle?'

Crisp Flavours Rejected by Scots

Despite the constant warnings about the dangers of over-salty diets, Scots just refuse to abandon their love affair with the potato crisp. Every year, we munch our way through millions of packets. Over the years, however, even we Scots had to draw a line somewhere. Among the rejects, for reasons of bad taste, insult to national pride or just downright pansyness, have been the following flavours:

Haggis
Hedgehog
Strawberry Fool
Mince Pie
Apricot

Where are All the Gaels?

The gradual disappearance of Gaelic from Lowland Scotland is illustrated by the fact that the last native speaker in Carrick, Ayrshire, Margaret MacMurray, died when Robert Burns was still a baby. Figures from the 2001 census made difficult reading for folk in the Gaelic lobby – only 58,552 Scots aged three and over spoke Gaelic at the time of the survey. This showed a drop of almost 7500 in ten years and it is the first time the figure has fallen below 60,000. Possibly the most interesting statistic from the census was the fact that 45 per cent of Gaelic speakers now live outwith the Highlands and Islands. The aim of the activists has consistently been to seek legislation to recognise Gaelic as a national language.

Here are some sayings you are unlikely to find in any of the Gaelic phrasebooks!

Tha riaghaltas na h-Alba a' cur taic thlachdmhor ri leasachadh na Gàidhlig
The Scottish Executive fully supports Gaelic development

Bha trì mìosan de dh'aimsir àluinn, samhraidh againn
We've had three months of glorious summer weather

Tha eaconomaidh nan Eilean Siar cho fallain ri ròn na mara
The economy of the Western Isles is as healthy as sea lions

Tha saoghal na Gàidhlig a' cur an làn earbsa ann am Bòrd na Gàidhlig
The Gaelic world has every confidence in the Gaelic Board

*Chòrd farpais nan òran ainmichte aig a' Mhòd Nàiseanta
Rìoghail rium*
I enjoyed the Prescribed Song competition at the Royal
National Mod

Bheir mi an aire dh'an rud a tha seo le ceud cabhaig
This matter will be treated with the utmost urgency

By the way, there are just eighteen letters in the Gaelic alpha-
bet. Wisely, I reckon, the Gaels have learned to live without
J, K, Q, V, W, X, Y and Z.

Scrugging Yer Bunnet

Long before steel helmets came into use, Highlanders used to
'scrug' or soak their bonnets in a stream. The soaking headgear
would, it was claimed, blunt a sword blow. Aye, well, dodging
the blow would still seem the more sensible option.

Making an Impression

Meet Anne Bristow-Kitney for whom Scotland meant nothing
special until she woke up one morning, a few years ago,
speaking, in her own words, like an extra from *Dr Finlay's
Casebook*. She had suffered a stroke and one outcome of the
event was that she was affected by Foreign Accent Syndrome.

None of her family or close friends is Scottish. She was
brought up in Chelsea, Cheltenham and Gloucestershire.
Experts explain that this case is unusual but not unique and
involves damage to the links to speech control centres – a form
of organic brain damage. The brain had picked out the Scottish

accent at random and it meant Anne was mimicking some-one she had met, perhaps only briefly, years before. The expectation, in such cases, is that the normal accent will gradually return. But, for a wee while, Anne knew what it meant to be an honorary Scot – a rare privilege for sooth-moothers.

And finally, we all know that, throughout the world, it is a given that two negatives make a positive but are you surprised to learn that Scots is the only language in which two positives can make a negative? Confused? Don't be – here's a wee example of how it works:

STATEMENT: Jim Hewitson's Scottish Miscellany *will make an important contribution to the understanding of the nature of Scottishness. It is an admirable, even classic, collection of social history, combining sensitive scholarship with an artful, witty, elegant and lucid style. This is a distinguished, significant, even epoch-making piece of esoterica.*

RESPONSE: *Aye! Right!*

INDEX

Alternative Medicines, 151, 158–9
Amputation, 75
Anthems, 133–5, 149–50
Antonine's Wall, 79
Art, 173
Assault Weapons, 181

Ba' Game, 54–5
Bad Habits, 40–45
Bagpipes see Pipe Bands and
  Dedications
Banking, 74–6
Baptism, 8
Barbour, John, 60
Bastard Verdict, 69–70
Bastian, 8
Beggars, 143–4
Beregonium, 154–6
Birds, 123, 168–9
Books, titles of, 52
Bracken, 157
Brechin, Randy Lass o', 21;
  big burghers of, 84
Bruce, Robert, 72
Buddishm, 138

Caber-tossing, 122
Candles, 121
Cars, 8–9
Cattle Ripping, 122
Censorship, 112–13
Choices, 40–5
Clans, 7, 73, 106, 138
Clubbing, 160–61
Coastline, 172
Complaints, 35
Comyn, John, 72
Cooking, 21, 25, 91, 128, 132, 142, 145,
  150, 156
Country and Western Music, 152–3
Covenanters' Grace, 53
Culloden, 38–9
Curry, 137

Declaration of Arbroath, 56–8
Dedications, 16–17
Disguises, 130–31
Dumbarton Castle, 128
Dumfries, dignified dwellers of, 86

Dundee, 39
Dunfermline, distinguished
  dudes of, 85

Edinburgh Festival Fringe, 15, 94–5
Edward I, 126
Eerie Events, 67
Eggs, 129
Elephants, 162
Employment, 118, 184–5
Exclamations, 110, 172
Exposure, 19

Fairies, 110, 114
Fickleness, 124
Fiery Crosses, 7
Flowers, 133
Flynn, Errol, 21
Folklore, 90–91
Football, 80–2, 126
Foreigners, 40–45
Forres, famous folk of, 84
France, 83
Freedom, 60

Gaelic, 124–5, 188–9
Genealogy, 107–108
Glencoe, Massacre of, 109
Goats, 8, 96

Haddington, historical honchos of, 86
Haggis, 103–105
Hallowe'en, 66–7
Hamesuckin', 151
Hamilton, Gavin, 88–9
Handel G. F., 122
Hare, 117–18
Heather Ale, 96–8
Highland Games, 122
Hillwalking, 127
Historical Figures, 40–45
History, 14
Home Guard, 7
Horseshoes, 11
Hunting see Kelpies

Illumination, 121
Insects, 8–9
Insults, 32–4

Inverness, important inhabitants of, 85
Invisibility, 123

Jacobites, 148; *see also* Culloden
James I, 59

Kelpies, 71–2
Keys, 53
Killiecrankie, Battle of, 49
Kingship, 26–7
Knox, John, 92, 141

Language, 113, 189–90
Law/Lawyers, 69–70
Legends, 14
Lies/Lying, 40–45, 87
Literature, 166–7
Lobsters, 99–101
Loch Lomond, 114

Macrae, Duncan, 13
McGinn, Matt, 35
Mary, Queen of Scots, 12
Measures, 165
Mistaken Identity, 95
Mountains, 127
Movies, 12
Multiple Foreskins *see* Relics
Murray, Chic, 115–16
Museums, 28–30
Music Hall, 92

Nairn, noted natives of, 85
Names, 18, 61–5, 174–5
Nessie, 40–45
Nudity, 19

Omens, 28
Orkney, 111
Ossian, 124

Pearls, 46–8
Pie Culture, 146; *see also* Clubbing
Pipe Bands, 170–71
Potato Crisps, 187
Precedence, 146–7
Proverbs, 124–5
Public Speakers, 40–45

Relics, 68
Research, 162–4

Roadkill, 9
Roundabouts, 102–103
Rutherglen, renowned residents of, 84
Rhymer, Thomas the, 121

St Magnus 68
Satan, 10–11
Scott, Sir Walter 80–82, 132
Sex, 11
Shetland *see* Up-Helly-A'
Shirts, 15
Shotts, 86
Simpsons, The, Wullie the
   groundsman, 20
Sinclair, Sir John, 178–80
Slavery, 187
Smiths, 61–5
Social Gaffes, 8
Stair Family, 77–8
Stirling, stupendous citizens of, 84
Stuarts, 186
Substitutes, 154

Talent Spotting, 59
Tam o' Shanter, 112–13
Tartan, 79
Tattooing, 182–3
Titanic *see* Urban Myths
Toasts, 93
Towns, 177
Town-twinning, 119–20
Transport, 40–45, 66–7
Tubes, 136
Turro' Show, 176
TV Newsreaders, 50–51

Union, Treaty of, 21, 22–4
Up-Helly-A', 36–7
Urban Myths, 176
Urine, 82, 148, 157

Veterinary Medicine, 151

Water Spirits *see* Kelpies
Weather, 139–42
Wee Cock Sparra, the, 12–13
Witchcraft, 117–18
Women, 40–45
Words, 52